"WALKING THROUGH WALLS is a uniquely illuminating and deeply penetrating journey to personal healing. Dr. Lee Jampolsky has tapped into the key principles of relieving inner pain, and presents them in a reader-friendly and practical way. I am moved and inspired by his message. Please embrace these great ideas and put them into action. Your life will change, and so will the world you see."

—Alan Cohen, author of *I Had All the Time*

"Dr. Lee Jampolsky's new book is wonderful, helpful, inspiring, practical, and easy to use. It will certainly help readers to realign with their true selves so that they may fully participate in their purpose as they journey through life."

—John Gray, author of *Men Are From Mars,*
Women Are From Venus

"WALKING THROUGH WALLS is a realistic prescription for stepping through the barriers of our perceived limitations into the lives we long to live. Dr. Jampolsky brings a lifetime of wisdom, gleaned through his recovery from addiction as a young man, his successful career as a psychologist and, finally, his commitment to spiritual life. WALKING THROUGH WALLS is as practical as it is transformative and hopeful."

—Hal Zina Bennett, author of *Writing Spiritual Books:*
A Bestselling Writer's Guide to Successful Publication

D0099333

"Dr. Jampolsky's eight-week program in practical spirituality is both inspiring and transforming. His prayerful and compassionate approach to life is an antidote to our stressful times."

—Marianne Williamson, author of *The Gift of Change*

"This amazing book will help keep your moral compass pointed in the right direction. It's a vital step-by-step handbook for anyone wanting to lead a rich, successful, abundant and generous life. It's the new *Seven Habits of Highly Effective People*."

—Jason Jennings, author of *Less Is More* and
It's Not the Big that Eat the Small It's the Fast that Eat the Slow

"Most books inspire us for a few days, and then the habits of a lifetime take over again. Dr. Lee Jampolsky describes a potent way to permanently transform those old, self-defeating habits into the self-restoring traits that bring permanent peace of mind."

—Dickson C. Buxton, author of *Lessons in Leadership and Life:
Secrets of Eleven Wise Men*

WALKING
THROUGH
WALLS

*Practical Spirituality
for an
Impractical World*

~

LEE JAMPOLSKY, PH.D.

CELESTIAL ARTS
Berkeley | Toronto

CELESTIAL ARTS

PO Box 7123
Berkeley, CA 94707
www.tenspeed.com

Distributed in Australia by Simon & Schuster Australia, in Canada by Ten Speed Press Canada, in New Zealand by Southern Publishers Group, in South Africa by Real Books, and in the United Kingdom and Europe by Airlift Book Company.

Cover and text design by Brad Greene / Greene Design
Cover photography supplied by photos.com

Library of Congress Cataloging-in-Publication Data on file with the publisher

ISBN 1-58761-218-6

First printing 2005

Printed in the United States of America

1 2 3 4 5 6 7 8 9 10 – 09 08 07 06 05 04

For Robin Dawn

To know one is loved transforms a once insurmountable wall
into little more than a thin veil.
Thank you for this gift.

Acknowledgments

Though there are usually many people to acknowledge in each of my books, in actuality this particular book had a small circle. I think this is because the content is so close to my heart. This book came into being because those at Celestial Arts, especially Veronica Randall and Jo Ann Deck, believed in the material. It has been a joy to work with you both. As always, those closest to me have inspired me, so a special thanks to my daughters Jalena and Alexandra, and to my partner Robin.

CONTENTS

THE LANGUAGE OF SPIRITUALITY

≈

THIS BOOK WILL TAKE YOU on a spiritual journey by way of the written word. Though words are effective tools, they have their limitations. One being that, depending on your cultural background, and life experience, spiritual language can be read as religious dogma. At the onset I want to address this, and explain my use of the terms "God," "Spirit," and "Higher Power," which I have chosen for no other reason than they reflect my own inner dialogue. None of these words promote a singular or closed belief system. Rather, all point to the common thread that runs through all spiritual traditions and religions: That there is a power greater than ourselves that lovingly guides us on our path through life. I refer to the state of awareness when we are in line with this power as God-centered thinking, and when we are not, as fear-based thinking. I use the term "ego" not in the Freudian sense, rather I define it as the part of the mind that is fearful because it believes it is separate from God and the rest of humanity. The ego and fear-based thinking are synonymous.

FOREWORD

～

THOMAS MERTON ONCE WROTE, "There is no way to tell people that they are walking around shining like the sun." Perhaps it is simply that I like a challenge, so I am going to give it a try. I have written this book to show you, or at least to plant the seed within you, that you are already shining like the sun. All you need are a few essential tools to help you along a spiritual path toward happiness and success, however you define them.

Though we may wish to believe that disadvantaged circumstances, lack of opportunity, or plain bad luck are what get in the way of our success and happiness, the walls that we come up against in life are almost always made with, or reinforced by, our own thoughts.

Because I am a psychologist, you may conclude my next suggestion will be, "All you need to do is change your thinking in order to achieve more success and live a happier life." While I have found such uplifting thoughts to be helpful, I also find them incomplete. Positive thinking can certainly create a happier atmosphere in which to live your life, but I am interested in more. Much more. I want for you and for myself the deeply profound joy, peace, and success that come from the discovery of purpose, meaning, significance, faith, service, and love.

If you find yourself even periodically unhappy in your personal relationships, in your work and your home, you may believe that God and spiritual fulfillment are nowhere to be found anymore. Don't worry. This is where I began, and it is the place from which most people begin their spiritual journey. All that is necessary right now is the thought that maybe, just maybe, God has not left you all alone and isolated in a harsh and bewildering world. At this moment, just the tiniest spark of hope is more than enough.

Throughout my personal journey and in my previous work as a psychologist, I found that the issue of trust in a power greater than myself had to be addressed before any significant or meaningful change could occur. The truth about my own life, which has had its share of health, relationship, and career challenges, can be summed up in one statement:

WHENEVER I OVERCOME AN OBSTACLE AND LEARN A SPIRITUAL LESSON IN THE PROCESS, I DO SO BECAUSE I HAVE DECIDED TO PUT GOD IN CHARGE AND FOLLOW HIS DIRECTION.

Trust in God was, is, and always will be the core issue for me. As you develop trust in God and in your self, you will be able to walk through the walls that have impeded your personal and career success.

First, let me be more specific as to what I mean by "trust." We tend to think trust is about whether or not others have proven themselves to be trustworthy, or about the personal dishonesty we may feel guilty about having committed in the past. Although this level of trust is important, it is not what this book is about. My purpose is to help you come to know that *you are trustworthy* and that *God is trustworthy.* This means knowing that we are each fully capable and loving human beings, and that God created us in His loving image. It means acknowledging the fear that limits us. It means acknowledging God's love that sets us free. Trust in God means you will not impose limitations on yourself or others. Trust in God means you will always see growth and healing as available choices. It means you will stop blaming others. It means you will begin to embrace all of who you are.

The type of trust you will develop in yourself will lead you to recognize the interconnectedness of all life. In short, when you decide to trust by turning your life in the direction of God, your inner guidance and outward actions are in accord. And, you will live in harmony with your self, with others, and within your environment.

There can be purpose and meaning in everything we do, (even in the tasks we don't find so appealing), in all situations (no matter what challenges they present), and in all people who enter our lives (even the ones we may not like). These are the "walls," the hidden gems we will learn to recognize as the invaluable lessons, the precious teachers that are here for us.

To walk through walls with God at your side, just stride ahead. You will soon be walking through them because when you learn to trust God, the walls will cease to exist.

Your 8-Week Program

~

IT WILL BE OF BENEFIT TO YOU—at home, in the work-place, and in your personal life—to turn your attention to the primary spiritual traits that rest on, and enhance your trust in, God. These are the aspects of yourself that will launch the direction of your life, set the quality of the way you live, and determine the success and happiness of who you are. There is nothing lofty or theoretical about this program. It is practical spirituality that you can use right away.

Over the next eight weeks you will be focusing on develop-ing one trait per week. The traits are honesty, tolerance, gen-tleness, joy, defenselessness, generosity, patience, and open-mindedness. They provide the foundation for living a God-cen-tered, abundant, successful life. The lessons that follow are designed to help remove the blocks that keep us from trusting God and guide you to the depths of your inner self and your relationship with your Higher Power. Picking up this book was no accident. You are ready to transform your life and work. I suggest you proceed with this transformation by reading the short passages on each trait and then practicing the daily lessons that follow.

In this program you will spend one dedicated and disciplined week on each spiritual trait. Each trait is presented in a discussion, followed by two lessons. Each lesson should be practiced for three days, as this has been found to be the minimum amount of time needed to absorb the lesson and incorporate it into your life. Additionally, there is a Sunday lesson that remains constant throughout the program. Your weekly schedule is:

- ❧ Each **Sunday:** Practice the Sunday Lesson presented on page xix.

- ❧ **Monday, Tuesday,** and **Wednesday:** Practice the first lesson for the trait of the week.

- ❧ **Thursday, Friday,** and **Saturday:** Practice the second lesson.

This is important. Try to stick to this rhythm. If you should forget, please don't quit or berate yourself. Simply pick up wherever you would be for that given day in order to stay on track. If you are beginning the program on a day other than Sunday or Monday, practice the Sunday Lesson continuously until you arrive at the schedule outlined above. For example, if you begin on a Wednesday, practice the Sunday Lesson on

Wednesday through Sunday, and then start Lesson One on the following Monday.

The purpose of each lesson is to aid you in the applied practice of the theoretical material that is presented. Theory and explanation are helpful, but alone they are insufficient. Spiritual principles must be put into action or they remain only ideas. So, to get the most out of the lessons I encourage you to practice the lessons in the following manner:

1. Each morning, soon after rising, remind yourself of the important spiritual work you are doing. Remind yourself that nothing else is more important than this. Then, review the lesson for the day. As described earlier, practice one lesson over three days, and the Sunday Lesson on each and every Sunday. It is important that you find a quiet place to practice where you won't be distracted or disturbed. This may be easier said than done, but it is important. Relax, and spend about five minutes slowly reading the lesson. Try to keep it in the forefront of your mind. During your practice time concentrate on the lesson and try to let go of any distracting thoughts. If unwanted thoughts interrupt your concentration, simply acknowledge their presence and then let them go. If you find your mind wandering, calmly, but quickly, refocus on the lesson as soon as you realize you've wandered off. In the first weeks, you may need to do this many times before your mind becomes disciplined enough to stay focused.

2. Review the lesson for a few moments periodically throughout the day, preferably on the hour. Slowly and thoughtfully repeat the lesson to yourself. Keep in mind that it is not as important to apply the lesson to all people and all situations as it is to *make no exclusions*. Do not make exceptions. This will be especially useful in times of conflict. You may find it helpful to either carry the book with you, or to copy each lesson onto a 3 x 5 card and carry then in your purse or briefcase. Be creative. There are many ways to remind yourself to recall each lesson. For example, I have a vibrating alarm on my watch that I have set to go off each hour during the day.

3. In the evening, preferably right before retiring, review the lesson again. Also reread the discussion of the trait that appears before each lesson. Think about your day. Consider how the trait you are developing and the lesson for that day apply to the specific circumstances of your day. Was there a situation that was particularly difficult when you forgot to apply the lesson? Imagine how you could have applied the lesson to that situation. This will help you in the future. Remember, mistakes are to learn from, not to condemn yourself over.

No one will be the "perfect student" over the course of eight weeks. And that's fine. Perfection is not the goal. Intention is all that is asked. There will be times when you could have benefited from applying the lessons when you did not.

And there will be times when you'll forget the lessons entirely. For this reason, after completing all the lessons in the series, you may want to begin again and repeat the program, or perhaps just the traits you feel you need some extra work. It is best to maintain your practice as a continuum until you find yourself living the traits and applying the lessons consistently. Your daily practice consists of three parts:

1. Morning practice session.

2. An hourly review and application to specifics that arise during your day.

3. An evening review.

Enjoy each day's progress, and be grateful for every challenge that presents itself. Trust that with each challenge you are being presented with an opportunity to apply the traits you are learning. When appropriate, share with others the progress you are making and the benefits to your life. A key principle to practical spirituality is *you teach what you want to learn*. Thus, sharing with others will be of benefit to all.

SUNDAY LESSON

Because the spiritual traits set forth in this book entail a very different way of being in the world than the ego's fear-based thinking promotes, developing detachment will be immeasurably helpful. The Sunday Lesson is a two-step approach that is designed to be a life-long practice. Through repetition you will build a foundation for the other lessons by cleansing your mind of unwanted negative ideas and emotions and by honing your ability to direct your thoughts in a more conscious and therefore more positive way.

The Sunday Lesson accomplishes this by "watching" the mind at work with as little attachment as possible. Sit with your eyes closed and simply "observe" your thoughts as they arise with the same detachment with which you would watch cars whiz by on a freeway. As you observe each thought, categorize it as "negative" or "positive." (If you prefer, you can use other terms, such as "fear-based" or "God-centered." The description per se doesn't matter.) Then ask yourself, "Does this thought bring me happiness?" "Is this thought conducive to my peace of mind?" "Will this thought create actions on my part that bring happiness to others?" Each time you question the origin and outcome of a thought, you are training your mind to *observe, think, and choose.*

After a few minutes, jot down your thoughts and the categories you've placed them in. Doing this will help you more quickly recognize and restrain your negative thinking, and choose the God-centered thinking that allows the eight spiritual traits to flourish. Although this may be difficult at first, with a little practice you may find yourself enjoying the process and wanting to do it for longer periods.

As often as you can, remind yourself:

- Attachment to negative thoughts and emotions is what keeps me from being happy.

- Detachment from negative thoughts and emotions brings me closer to the happiness I desire and deserve.

- When I act, or react, from fear-based thinking, I create suffering for myself and others.

- When I choose to act, or react, from God-centered thinking, my choices create joy within me and for those around me.

- If I fail to identify my negative thoughts and emotions, I fail to recognize the source of my pain and thus perpetuate the endless cycle of blame.

- When I embrace my responsibility for my negative thoughts and emotions and choose to remain detached from them, I end the cycle of pain and blame.

- Fear-based thinking not only robs me of peace of mind, it causes many needless health problems.

- God-centered thinking not only promotes peace of mind, it enhances my good health.

- The extent to which I give in to negative thoughts and emotions is the degree to which I exclude the positive spiritual traits I wish to adopt.

❧ Every time I choose detachment from negative thoughts and emotions, I come closer to the positive spiritual traits I wish to adopt.

At a minimum, practice this lesson twice each Sunday. I also recommend you read and contemplate the list upon waking, at the noon hour, and before going to sleep.

～ HONESTY ～

ALTHOUGH YOU ARE RELUCTANT TO BELIEVE THAT YOUR OWN
ACTIONS AND ATTITUDES HAVE BEEN THE CAUSE OF YOUR
PAIN, EVENTUALLY YOU CANNOT IGNORE THIS CONFLICT.

—Tarthang Tulka, *Gesture of Balance*

CREATE AND MAINTAIN CONSISTENCY IN YOUR WORDS, THOUGHTS, AND ACTIONS.

Most of us tend to think of honesty in terms of words, and
that if you "tell the truth," you are being honest. But our definition of honesty needs to be broadened. Real honesty means
consistency between what you say, what you do, and what you
think. *A Course in Miracles* eloquently expands this idea:

> There is nothing you say that contradicts what you think or
> do; no thought opposes any other thought; no act belies your
> word; and no word lacks agreement with another. Such are

1

the truly honest. At no level are they in conflict with themselves. Therefore it is impossible for them to be in conflict with anyone or anything.

DON'T EXPECT OTHER PEOPLE TO CONGRATULATE YOU ON YOUR HONESTY.

In an earlier book, *Healing the Addictive Mind,* I discussed my addictions and how my life was affected by them. I remember the day, now over twenty-five years ago, when I finally decided to tell other people in my life about what I had been doing—the addictions, the secrecy, the dishonesty—and about my isolation. I had been seeing a psychologist for a number of months. We decided it would benefit my sobriety if I were to meet with the two people to whom I was most afraid to reveal my addiction: my father and my physician.

My doctor was a man with whom I had been very close. From the time I was fifteen until I turned twenty-one, he had always been an emotional anchor in my life. I knew that he cared for me deeply not only as a patient, but also as an individual. The problem was that I had been lying to him for years in order to get prescription pain medication. I also thought lying was the only way I could get emotional support. I had faked pain, purposely got into car accidents, and used many other methods of manipulation to continue to get drugs. At the same time, I felt tremendous guilt over this behavior. What I really wanted was understanding and love, but I did not know how to stop the vicious cycle of dishonesty I had created.

To compound the problem, when I met with my father and my doctor, I harbored the mistaken belief that all I needed to do was to "come clean," to be honest and tell them what had been happening. Then I would magically become understood, appreciated, and forgiven. I believed my confession was all that would be required of me.

To my surprise, however, meeting with them and telling them the truth was merely the first step in a long journey that eventually led to trust and honesty. I would learn that while having the intention of being honest is positive, it is the practice itself—consistently acting with integrity toward yourself, other people, the planet, and God—that truly leads to a life of simplicity, abundance, and peace.

On the day of my "confession," I remember being angry at my father and my doctor for not immediately congratulating me on the new direction my life was taking. Though supportive, they were, at the same time, upset and mistrustful of me; after all, I had been lying to them off and on for years. My doctor was quite angry, and he discontinued much of our professional and personal relationship. This was extremely painful for me. I don't think he really knew how much his friendship had meant in my life. I felt that being honest had resulted in losing my anchor to sanity. Honesty, I believed, had led to loss.

With continued self-exploration I realized what I really needed to do was to stop condemning myself and start forgiving myself. As my wish to deceive myself (and others) about who I was and what I was doing decreased, I found I was able to be gentler and more forgiving with myself. Forgiveness, in turn, allowed honesty to be born, for it is impossible to be honest and unforgiving at the same time. Try to remember the following:

FORGIVING YOURSELF AND OTHERS ALLOWS FOR DEEPER HONESTY.

TRUSTING IN YOUR HIGHER POWER LEADS TO DEEPER HONESTY.

But:

GUILT OVER THE PAST INHIBITS YOUR ABILITY TO BE HONEST.

FEAR OF THE FUTURE INHIBITS YOUR ABILITY TO BE HONEST.

To be unforgiving toward yourself or others you must be, in some way, condemning. Further, to condemn yourself or others is dishonest because it is not God-centered.

Any practice that is reflective of trusting your Higher Power is honest, even if it is hard to swallow or share with someone at the time. Don't be attached to what occurs when you express your honesty, as it may not always be welcomed. This is why true honesty takes courage, and true courage takes turning to your Higher Power for help. Always remember, any communication that places undo emphasis on guilt over the past or fear about the future is somewhat dishonest, because it is born from fear-based thinking.

Fear about the future is often based on fear of how someone will react to your honesty, or about loss that might come from your honesty. Know that if you are sure about your truth and that it is from your Higher Power, all will come out as it should in the long run. Trust that being true to yourself and your spiritual path is of the utmost importance in developing honesty. If you don't commit to this, don't expect to have the life that you want to create for yourself. If you were to choose one cause of a life of mediocrity, it would be lacking the courage or desire to be honest.

Thus, the most honest thing you can do is look at yourself and others not from the viewpoint of a judgmental past or a fearful future, but in the light of the present moment, where you are completely loved by God.

LESSON ONE

Forgiveness brings honesty and ends all conflict.

Today is the first of several lessons that will emphasize forgiveness. In order to bring honesty into your daily life, start by addressing the elements of conflict, which I define broadly as any state of mind other than the experience of serenity in the present moment. The first important realization within this lesson is: the conflicted mind cannot be truly honest. Remember this: The peace of God is your natural state; the absence of it indicates a form of internalized conflict and fear-based thinking.

Fear-based thinking tells you that when you are in conflict with yourself or someone else, the way out is to ask a lot of questions. If you look closely, the motivating force behind these questions is usually judgment, not understanding. If you are trying to be honest and resolve conflict from a God-centered approach, you will want to direct your mind toward understanding, not judgment. In order to understand and empathize, which always is the honest and God-centered way out of conflict, you need to ask only a few questions. It is helpful to remember in the pure honesty of God, He does not ask a lot of questions. Nor does He ask much of us other than to be willing to accept His love and to empathize with, understand, and love yourself and others. A dear friend of mine, Maria, sent me the simple words: God asks less and forgives more. If you do this with yourself and in your relationships you will actually be creating the deepest kind of honesty. Remember, then, your path to success and peace can be said in five words, even if you did nothing other than this you would live a full and loving life. The five words are:

ASK LESS AND FORGIVE MORE.

This being said, your mind will still ask questions, especially when you are in conflict with someone else or within yourself. Until your mind is disciplined enough to stop asking so many questions and simply accept and extend empathy, understanding, and love, the following questions will help you explore how you have dealt with conflict in the past. Paradoxically, they are designed to lead to not asking more questions. This is the beginning of the process of forgiving.

- Have you, at any time in your life, experienced conflict between another person and yourself but were afraid to address it?

- Do you ever do things you don't believe in order to avoid conflict?

- Have you ever internalized a conflict instead of addressing it, or blamed another person for it, or both at the same time?

- Do you ever "gloss over" a conflict in order to "keep the peace," but over time become resentful, if not bitter?

- Are you ever deceitful or manipulative with yourself or others in order to avoid conflict?

If you want honesty and all the benefits it will bring, conflict cannot be disguised, denied, evaded, hidden, or seen somewhere else. Rather, you need a new way of dealing with conflict, one that is God-centered and one that you can trust. Forgiveness is this gift.

Honesty implies resolving conflict, because to be authentically and fully honest is to accept your true and natural state, which is the peace of God. To resolve conflict you must be willing to recognize conflict whenever it presents itself. Then you must be willing to examine the thoughts that created the conflict. These will always come from fear-based thinking. Don't point your finger. Instead, get in the habit of looking at your own thoughts.

Becoming defensive is a good indicator that you are not God-centered in your thinking. God-centered thinking needs no defense. When you are able to lift all your defenses you will find empathy, understanding, and love. Remember that these are the hallmarks of honesty and defensiveness does not allow for honesty.

Today's lesson asks you to commit to changing the way you deal with conflict. It is devoted to identifying current conflicts and to healing them through the power of forgiveness. This is the path to honesty. Your conflicts could include old beliefs and feelings from childhood, as well as a situation that is taking place right now. Regardless, approach them in the same way.

Start a list of whatever you feel unforgiving about or have guilt about. Spend a fair amount of time with this. You may wish to leave it and come back to it throughout the day. Your first task will be to recognize issues that are unresolved in your life. Examples might include:

- I am angry with my father for leaving home.

- I don't like my job, but I stay because it is secure.

- There is tension between my spouse and me, though I pretend that everything is all right.

When you have completed your list ask yourself if you are

truly willing to deal with these issues differently than you have in the past. Doing so will mean committing yourself to resolving conflict rather than avoiding it or repeating the same actions even though they continue to prolong the conflict.

Begin by closing your eyes. Then, one by one, picture the person or people involved in each of the predicaments described on your list. Don't forget to include yourself. Repeat the following:

- Forgiveness is the way I choose to heal all conflict and all doubt.

- Holding onto anger is not going to help me.

- I forgive this by asking my Higher Power to help me let go all that gets in the way of His awareness, and I trust this will occur.

Remember that if you hold onto blame, the conflict cannot be resolved. Commit yourself today to the direct resolution of any conflict, new or old, that arises with another person. Do this by saying:

I WILL ASK LESS AND FORGIVE MORE.

Always remember and practice these seven words and you will always be on a spiritual path. With forgiveness as your foundation, you no longer have to be afraid to address the issues that so profoundly affect your life. Without fear, honesty happens.

LESSON TWO

Those who are honest hold no grievances.

In the preceding lesson you learned that forgiveness leads to peace because it is wholly honest. Today you will look at the other side of the equation: the fact that holding a grievance always leads to guilt and blocks spiritual growth. Guilt and shame are indicators of fear-based thinking, and this is a denial of the truth that is available to you in the present moment. Thus, guilt and shame take you away from the kind of insightful honesty that can transform your life.

It is a common misperception that if you do not hold grievances you won't be motivated to take action. Or, if you do not hold grievances you will be left unprotected and the previous painful circumstances from the past will repeat themselves. Remember this:

THAT WHICH LEADS TO SUCCESS AND HAPPINESS IS COMPASSIONATE ACTION THROUGH UNDERSTANDING AND SERVICE. LETTING GO OF GRIEVANCES IS THE FIRST STEP TOWARD CREATING THIS.

To want to know yourself by turning to God is how to become totally honest. You cannot truly know yourself as long as you hold on to your grievances; they are like heavy, rusted iron doors hiding the light of forgiveness from your mind.

Holding on to grievances means forgetting that the love of God is available to you right now. When you hold on to a grievance you allow fear-based thinking rule your life. Because fear-based thinking uses denial of God, blaming others, and self-condemnation as its primary tools, it is clearly dishonest. Today, it is vital that you see the effects that holding grievances has upon your life. When you clearly see this you will be sufficiently motivated to work toward letting them go. With the absence of grievances the path to your Higher Power is much more clear, and honesty flows naturally.

You may not realize it, but holding grievances means that you are denying that you are worthy of God's love. You cannot condemn another person and at the same time feel fully worthy yourself. The ego will argue that this is not the case, however. When you see the light of God in another person you see it in yourself. When you are too busy holding a grievance, you obscure the light of God within yourself and can't see it. When you hold on to grievances, you see yourself as split off from your Higher Power, and other people. In short:

HOLDING ON TO GRIEVANCES SHUTS YOU OFF FROM KNOWING YOURSELF, KNOWING OTHERS, AND KNOWING GOD.

The short form is that holding a grievance makes you unhappy. Giving even one grievance any power at all begins a whole series of attack thoughts—of blaming—which keep opportunity and honesty out of your grasp. Holding on to grievances is nothing short of denying God, and this is at the core of dishonesty with yourself. Remind yourself often:

WHEN YOU HOLD ON TO A GRIEVANCE YOU FORGET WHO YOU ARE.

WHEN YOU FORGIVE YOU WILL REMEMBER.

You may be reading this and thinking that you cannot possibly release all your grievances. Or, you may still believe that at least some of them are keeping you safe, and you don't want to let them all go. Letting go is simply a matter of motivation and belief.

Today your goal is to find out how you would feel without your grievances. If you succeed in doing so, even ever so slightly, you will never have a motivation problem again. You will never have to wonder if you want to be honest; it will even cease to be a question.

As with the previous lessons, begin today by searching your mind for people against whom you hold a major grievance. Next, look for minor grievances that you hold towards those you like, and even love. You will quickly see that there are few people towards whom you do not hold some kind of grievance. This is what makes you feel alone and gets in the way of true inner peace and quality relationships. Remind yourself:

I AM EITHER CHOOSING GRIEVANCES OR CHOOSING THE PATH OF GOD.

Today, determine to see each and every person you have a grievance with as your teacher, whether you know them well or not. One by one, say to them:

> I CHOOSE TO SEE YOU AS MY TEACHER, SO THAT
> THROUGH FORGIVENESS I MAY REMEMBER WHO I AM,
> WHO YOU ARE, AND WHO GOD IS.

With your eyes closed, spend about ten minutes envisioning yourself totally at peace with everyone. Pretend for a moment you are looking at the world with nothing but peace and compassion in your heart. Imagine you have a type of "celestial amnesia" whereby you can remember no grievance of any kind against anyone. Remind yourself that you are perfectly safe without your grievances. Feel the safety that surrounds you as you pray, gently repeating the following words:

> PLEASE LIFT ALL GRIEVANCES FROM MY TIRED MIND.

Believe that nothing can harm this peace of mind. You may find it helpful to say to yourself:

THE TRULY HONEST HOLD NO GRIEVANCES.

AS I TURN OVER ALL MY GRIEVANCES TO MY HIGHER POWER

I WILL KNOW I AM PERFECTLY SAFE.

KNOWING I AM SAFE, I CAN BE HONEST.

Also, quickly apply this lesson whenever any grievance arises against anyone during the course of the day. It does not matter whether that person is physically present. Say to yourself:

I MAKE THE COMMITMENT TO ADD NOT ONE MORE TOXIC GRIEVANCE TO MY MIND.

IF I MISTAKENLY DO, LET ME TURN TO MY HIGHER POWER ONCE AGAIN AND ASK:

PLEASE LIFT ALL GRIEVANCES FROM MY TIRED MIND.

～ TOLERANCE ～

AND LET THERE BE NO PURPOSE IN FRIENDSHIP SAVE THE
DEEPENING OF THE SPIRIT.

—Kahlil Gibran, *The Prophet*

REFRAIN FROM NEGATIVE JUDGMENT.

Not long ago I received what appeared to be an invitation. In
festive calligraphy it read:

God is throwing a very special party in the grand ballroom.

All of the people in the ballroom will be His special guests.

When you arrive, how will you treat His guests?

In a clever way (the original idea came from the fourteenth-
century poet Hafiz of Shiraz) it pointed to the tolerance it
would behoove us all to develop while we are here at the party

of life. Indeed, each of us is God's special guest and, despite what we may think, nobody gets to crash His party!

I believe most of us share the desire for a tolerant and compassionate approach to life, even if we are not always consciously aware of it. The trick is to bring this desire to the forefront of our thinking, especially during difficult or stressful times. To accomplish this, keep in mind:

- To judge is to be intolerant, and to be intolerant is to be dishonest.

- Each of us is inherently worthy of God's love.

- Each of us has the inherent ability to forgive.

- Judgment and intolerance deny the truth that God wishes you to see. In lieu of the truth, you hold yourself to be superior (if you are judging others), or inferior (if you are judging yourself).

- Because, in truth, you are neither superior nor inferior to your fellow human beings, to judge and be intolerant assumes a position you do not have.

In developing tolerance I have found it helpful to have role models. Without them, tolerance remained a distant concept for me. Two such role models in my life are the Dalai Lama and the late Mother Teresa. Each demonstrates that it is possible to walk through life with a minimum of judgment and an abundance of tolerance. Each faced great adversity. Each used an approach to those challenges that included the practice of tolerance. I remind myself that in terms of the potential within each of us, these two people are no different from anyone else. They are simply human beings who have chosen to adopt a perception of the world that is love-based rather than fear-based, and sought solutions based upon this choice. There is no reason that you and I cannot do the same in the context of our lives and the problems we encounter.

ARE YOU A NEGATIVE SANTA? DO YOU ONLY MAKE LISTS OF WHAT'S WRONG AND CHECK IT TWICE?

Be honest. Are you the kind of person who keeps detailed inventories on all the ways in which your spouse, in-laws, friends, boss, colleagues, etc., are intolerant and critical? (Do you notice any irony in the fact that you may be intolerant of other people's intolerance?) As with all of the traits that rest on trust, the best way to receive tolerance from others is to develop tolerance in yourself. It is a magical solution: When you refrain from being judgmental, and turn to God, the world immediately becomes a much safer place for you. Just as tolerance breeds tolerance, judgment and intolerance breeds judgment and intolerance. If I say, "I will be caring towards you as soon as you are more tolerant of me," I keep myself stuck in fear-based thinking. It is when we extend tolerance through caring and empathy, rather than waiting for it to come to us first, that mutual consideration becomes possible in your life. Remember a simple fact:

JUDGMENT AND INTOLERANCE WITHOUT SELF-DELUSION IS IMPOSSIBLE.

When I forget this fact I fall back into believing that holding judgmental thoughts toward myself and others can be positive. Why? Because it means I'm being fiercely honest about who I am and who you are. But nothing could be further from the truth. Judgment and intolerance *create* deception, rather than reveal it. They actually obscure our vision of ourselves, others, and God.

God-centered thinking reflects the truth about who you are—that you are completely held in love and tenderness by God. Fear-based thinking, and the judgment and intolerance that result from it, are based on fear, which is illusion based on the past—a past that is over and finished. This means that judgment is really self-deception. God's love and tenderness escape your awareness and fear fills your mind. When you view yourself and others through the eyes of God's love you do not need to "try" to be tolerant, it will come naturally.

INTOLERANCE IMPLIES A LACK OF TRUST IN YOUR HIGHER POWER.

IT COMES FROM ARROGANCE AND UNWILLINGNESS TO EMBRACE THE MOMENT AS IT IS.

Without trust in your Higher Power, intolerance is inevitable. It traps you in a fearful dream that the ego convinces you is real. If you want to learn the lessons Spirit has to offer, you must be willing to relinquish judgment. Judgment destroys honesty, breeds intolerance, and does away with trust in your spiritual path.

DEVELOP THE DESIRE TO BE TOLERANT.

I do not condone behavior that is obviously wrong, such as oppression or the taking of a life. Rather, tolerance is the kind of thinking that comes as you align yourself with God rather than your ego as you look at the world and the diverse people and views that abound within it. Tolerance is a facet of love and compassion. Thus, it is a natural extension of your spiritual path. However, thanks to fear-based ways of thinking the world is full of intolerance, perhaps more so now than ever before. It is important for each one of us to do our part to change this. The first step is to develop the desire to be tolerant with yourself and others.

Each day I focus in on my desire to be tolerant with other people. Intolerance can be so sneaky in my mind. Without warning I find myself deeply entrenched in thinking that *my* way is the *only* way. When piloting a helicopter, I rely on a simple but effective visual aid—several small strings attached to the "windshield" that show me the flow of the air when the craft is hovering or in slow flight. The strings communicate subtle but important aerodynamic changes *before* they may actually be experienced, and thus allow me to make continuous adjustments for a safe flight. Similarly, I like to think of my personal intolerances as indicators that something in my thinking or perception needs adjusting. If I fail to react quickly with positive adjustments, things tend to go from bad to worse pretty darn quick, just like in the helicopter. Thus, the moment I catch myself being impatient with or reacting intolerantly toward someone I try to remind myself that if I am judging or blaming, an adjustment to my thinking is needed.

The "degree" of my intolerance might seem inconsequential; however, I have found that *any* lack of tolerance tends to snowball rather quickly. There is no judgmental thought or intolerant action, no matter how small or seemingly insignificant that does not block the awareness of your Higher Power. Decide to make a commitment to catch yourself when you become impatient and intolerant. It is amazing how having a commitment simply to move *in the direction* of understanding, empathy, and tolerance allows your whole life to shift. You begin to glimpse spiritual truths that were always there but you couldn't see. And you stop perceiving obstacles to God that were never there. It is a gift to feel the awareness of God flow into your heart when on the day before you might have been closed-minded. I suggest that such a shift in focus is possible in *all* of our relationships, *all* of the time, be they personal or professional, intimate or global. It is a matter of choice and discipline. I invite you to make the following commitment:

I WILL SEE ANY SIGN OF INTOLERANCE AS A MESSAGE THAT I HAVE DRIFTED AWAY FROM PUTTING GOD FIRST IN MY LIFE. I COMMIT TO REMEDY THIS AS SOON AS I SEE IT.

Do this by repeating a simple prayer:

Dear God,

Help me to see this differently. **Replace** the tension
of intolerance with the calm of empathy
and understanding.

~ *Amen*

A commitment to tolerance does not mean the things that
bother you should not be addressed. It does mean that uncomfortable issues are discussed and that such discussions are motivated by the desire to communicate with understanding and
empathy rather than judgment and self-righteousness.

LESSON THREE

**I will spend today practicing tolerance
and compassion.**

This pledge is a commitment to your spiritual path. Directing your mind in this way allows tolerance to illuminate a path
to deeper understanding of yourself and the world.

Remember this today:

WITH FEAR, I AM DEFENSIVE AND JUDGMENTAL; WITH
DEFENSIVENESS AND JUDGMENT, I AM FEARFUL.

Conversely:

WITH UNDERSTANDING, I AM TOLERANT; WITH TOLERANCE, I AM UNDERSTANDING.

Decide today that there is simply no room in your life for judgment and intolerance. By doing so you make room for understanding and tolerance. This is the only thing you need to concentrate on today. It is more important than anything else.

In today's lesson you seek to know the difference between imprisonment and freedom. When you were judgmental and intolerant in the past, you may have thought you were defending your freedom and independence. In fact, all you were doing was tightening the shackles around your heart, locking out the love of God and perhaps people dear to you.

Beyond teaching you that you are separate from God, fear-based thinking does not know what it is trying to teach you. Its only expertise is confusion. When you listen to the chatter of your ego telling you to judge, it is like listening to gossip. The ego is nothing. It is based upon fear and insecurity, and only false perception can follow—just like gossip.

You have free will. You can choose to be free in fearlessness and surrounded by the love of God, or imprisoned by fear and judgment. Today, exercise your power of decision. Begin by closing your eyes and thinking of all of the things you are intolerant of, all of the judgments that you hold. Notice that whatever you are intolerant of is almost always wrapped in fear. Spend about five minutes considering this, and be as specific as you can. Then say to yourself:

THESE FEARS AND JUDGMENTS HAVE NOTHING TO DO WITH WHO I AM, OR WHO OTHERS ARE. TODAY, I WILL SEEK THE TRUTH BY THE PRACTICE OF TOLERANCE. I WILL SPEND TODAY PRACTICING TOLERANCE AND COMPASSION.

Practicing tolerance does not mean that you don't address the things you are fearful about, or that may bother you. Rather, it is by consciously deciding to turn your fears and concerns over to your Higher Power that you will become empowered. When you seek to explore what you don't understand and practice tolerance for diverse views you are finally free to *effectively* address your concerns. This is because you won't be sidetracked by insecurities and intolerances that really don't matter.

Because intolerance and impatience are joined in your mind, ceasing your preoccupation with and anxiety over the future greatly reduces both impatience and intolerance. As you learn to utilize your Higher Power and trust the future, you will begin to recognize what is within your ability to change and what is not. Acceptance of yourself and others comes streaming into your life, as sunlight streams into a dark room. This can be summed by saying:

IT IS THROUGH ACCEPTANCE OF GOD IN THE PRESENT MOMENT THAT I WILL FIND TOLERANCE.

The day has come to decide to approach yourself and other people *without* blame and *with* the desire to understand. Whenever feelings arise from judgment, blame, or intolerance towards yourself or others, say:

I WILL NOT IMPRISON MYSELF TODAY. TODAY, I WILL PRACTICE TOLERANCE AND COMPASSION.

LESSON FOUR
My fault-finding and doubt injure me.

Today is a continuation of yesterday's lesson. One of the primary mistakes we can make is believing that always looking for what is wrong or lacking—in ourselves, in other people, in our relationships, in our work, with anything and everything that comes our way—will bring us what we want and make the world a safe and happy place for us. This is the opposite of living a spiritually based life. Remember, the primary reason to abandon a spiritual focus in daily life and become a fault-finder is because we doubt the power of God in our lives.

Today is devoted to remembering that you are moving along on the path toward a fuller awareness of your Higher Power. Instead of being a fault-finder and filled with doubt, you will look for the light of God in all.

It is not surprising that fault-finding has become an epidemic in our culture. People who are over-stressed, rushed, and take no time for reflection or stillness tend to become compulsive fault-finders and chronic doubters in the power of a spiritual path. They see what is wrong or lacking, because they believe it will bring them something different. Further, they believe that finding fault is a hallmark of high intelligence. Most of us, to some extent, fall into this trap of the ego. Traits such as faith and forgiveness are then seen as naive beliefs of the less intelligent. Finding fault in yourself and others, and doubting the power of God, are kissing cousins within the family of fear-based thinking.

Conversely, people who take time for quiet contemplation, meditation, and prayer tend to be able to see through more patient and loving eyes. They see opportunities rather than obstacles. Today, you make yourself one of these people by deciding to put a stop to fault-finding and fear-based doubt. The only "healthy doubt" is when your Higher Power begins to help you question your fear-based thinking. In this case, doubt serves as a bridge to a God-centered life.

Begin by repeating out-loud the principle below several times. Then, with your eyes closed, contemplate its application to your life:

YOU MAKE YOURSELF A PRISONER WHEN YOU FIND FAULT AND DOUBT THE POWER OF GOD.

FORGIVE AND YOU ARE FREED. FORGIVE AND YOU WILL SEE ENDLESS OPPORTUNITY.

Practice this, and you will discover opportunity where others see only obstacles.

Why would you want to injure anyone, or for that matter yourself? Why would you limit your potential in any way? When you are intolerant, a fault-finder, and a doubter this is what you are doing. Today, you begin your healing. You do this by consciously letting go of your condemning and limiting thoughts. As you know, physical wounds that are not cleaned will not heal. In the same way, your mind cannot be healed until you clean it of intolerance, fault-finding, and doubt. And as always, forgiveness provides the means by which you cleanse your mind. Today is devoted to halting the habit of fear-based thinking in its tracks and replacing it with the God-centered habit of forgiveness.

Forgiveness is the gentle "letting go" that allows all notions of lack, disaster, loss, doubt, and judgment to disappear, or at least lessen their hold on your mind. Intolerance, finding fault, and harboring doubt yield unforgiving thoughts that need to be brought into the light of God-centered thinking.

Even when you hold irrational thoughts and doubts, the stillness of God remains. Even when you continue to hurt yourself, God is fully loving and forgiving, and waiting for you to turn away from the old habit of fault-finding and open your heart to His presence.

Help pave the way to freedom today. Any time you become aware of feelings other than perfect tranquility and tolerance, say to yourself:

I MAKE MYSELF A PRISONER WHEN I FIND FAULT AND DOUBT THE POWER OF GOD.

FORGIVE AND I AM FREED. FORGIVE AND I WILL SEE OPPORTUNITY.

Decide, today, to wait no longer.

~ GENTLENESS ~

WHEN YOU EXPRESS GENTLENESS AND PRECISION IN YOUR ENVIRONMENT, THEN REAL BRILLIANCE AND POWER CAN DESCEND ONTO THAT SITUATION.

—Chögyam Trungpa, *Shambala*

THE WEAKNESS OF ATTACK IS NO MATCH FOR THE POWER OF GENTLENESS.

Gentleness is like a morning breeze that softly awakens you to the new day. Gentleness never employs force; it gets its power instead from yielding. It is not necessarily passive: its strength is derived from persistence. Gentleness nourishes you like a light spring rain, washing away your old judgmental thoughts and leaving only the radiance of the Now.

The ego once again uses the weapons of guilt and shame to convince you that gentleness is a sign of weakness instead of a sign of strength. The mind that holds on to guilt cannot in the same moment trust in God; and experiencing the peace of God becomes very unlikely. How can you adopt a genuine attitude of gentleness toward yourself while believing that you are guilty or shameful? You cannot, because guilt and shame tell you to be hard on yourself and other people. Judgment, shame, and guilt create a mind that has bars locking gentleness and serenity out.

To the mind that is guilty, the fear of attack lurks everywhere. And when you are expecting attack at any moment, gentleness is a luxury you cannot afford.

Fear-Based Thinking:

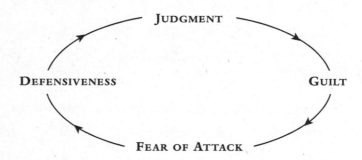

God-Centered Thinking:

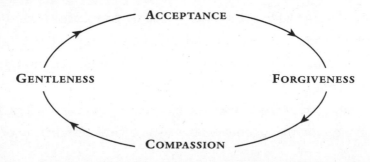

Laura had been in a series of unsuccessful relationships with men. Though she was a very attractive woman in her late thirties, during our first visits her thick, dark hair half-covered her face, as though she were peeking around a curtain to see if it was safe to come out. She seemed to use her smile to keep a safe distance between herself and me, and never actually expressed her feelings about anything. I remember that by the time she left the first session her sadness lingered in the air.

My work with Laura centered on developing trust, and the path toward trust is the path of gentleness. When Laura began being gentle with herself, she transformed her guardedness and distance with people—and her Higher Power—into a genuine and powerful presence.

Laura's father was a very talented and respected architect in a small community where he was looked upon as intelligent, hard working, and a true "family man." In reality, at home he was critical, self-absorbed, and verbally abusive. It was difficult for Laura to reveal that her father had made many sexual gestures towards her throughout her adolescence. Because he had not physically molested her, she assumed there was no "real" abuse and felt that she could not tell anyone about it. By repeatedly reasserting he never touched her, she minimized the importance of his behavior and of her own feelings about it. Laura learned to be very guarded at home. She never knew when an unwanted advance would occur.

Midway through our work together, Laura often mentioned how much she had progressed, stating that she had become very good at protecting herself rather than being a victim. This self-protection did indeed represent progress: Laura was more able to refrain from involving herself in relationships—especially with men—that were not right for her. Previously, if someone wanted to date her or spend time with her, she had felt obligated to say yes.

At the same time, however, she still felt unsafe, and believed that there was no safety in God. Although her life was certainly improving, she was still very guarded and always feared the "demands" made by other people. With fear and guardedness as the primary ways she operated in the world, gentleness towards herself and others was still absent.

YOU CAN MAKE A LOT OF PROGRESS IN LIFE, EVEN HAVE A VERY OUTWARDLY SUCCESSFUL LIFE, AND STILL LACK THE IMPORTANT TRAIT OF GENTLENESS.

Being on guard and protecting herself had allowed Laura to survive her childhood. But as an adult these "survival tools" kept her from happiness because they left little room for her to turn to God, or to give or experience gentleness. In order to adopt an attitude of gentleness, she had to see that she was not, in fact, in need of constant protection, and was protected by a power much greater than she could ever imagine—a protection from a power greater than herself. As she was able to trust in her Higher Power more, Laura was able to experience the gentleness of God. This in turn allowed her to become more gentle with herself and others.

To further her progress she had to learn the difference between assertiveness and protection. Fear-based thinking tells us that we should fear the future. It proclaims that every negative thing that has happened to us will most likely occur again if we do not defend ourselves and have limitless self-made defenses. There is obviously little room for gentleness here. In contrast, God-centered thinking asserts that gentleness is a result of turning to our Higher Power in the moment. This is in stark contrast to being in protection mode that the ego claims is always needed. More specifically, the differences in messages sent by God-centered thinking and fear-based thinking in this regard are as follows:

Fear-Based Thinking:

- Look to the past, then project this fear-filled past onto the future.

- Guard yourself at all times, otherwise you will get hurt.

- Defend yourself and you will be safe.

God-Centered Thinking:

- Quiet your mind. Then turn to your Higher Power and ask, "What is right for me right now?"

- Be gentle and forgiving with yourself and others.

- Know that gentleness is the path to knowing God.

You may feel that these guidelines suggest you should never set limits or have boundaries, or that it is all right to let others walk all over you. This is *not* the message.

The one thing I know to be true as I travel my own spiritual path is that by consistently turning to my Higher Power for guidance, rather than returning to my guilt and shame-filled past, I have become more able to trust God. In turn, I am more able to trust my ability to assert myself, when necessary, and to know what is right for me in the moment. This allows me to let go of guardedness or self-protectiveness. As I place more trust in a gentle approach to life, toward myself, and toward others, I know I can handle any challenge, in the moment, should one arise. Developing a gentle yet assertive approach to life has given me confidence where I once only had fear and doubt.

Herein lies an important and fundamental difference between assertiveness and protection: Assertiveness is based on turning to your Higher Power in the present moment. It is a feeling of confidence, knowing that we can voice our feelings and opinions, and if needed, protect ourselves from harm in the most gentle way possible. Conversely, the attitude of protection is one of a constant fear that limits our ability to react in the moment, unencumbered by the past.

In the martial art of Seibukan Jujutsu there is a practice called *henka*. Henka is based on the concept of *kan,* a word that roughly translates as "intuition." Not until receiving my black belt did I fully grasp the concept of henka in action. A practitioner of henka takes all he or she knows about the totality of their being and applies it to conflict situations, learning to trust and implement skills without being on guard. In henka, the martial artist is relaxed, supple, and without fear, regardless of what may be coming their way, allowing for a reaction to the situation *as it is,* rather than from fear of what it might be.

As a student of the martial arts, one of my goals is to become very good at the attitude of henka in my daily life. When I am successful I am able to walk through my life with gentleness and confidence.

You cannot cause harm and find the gifts God offers you.

Intentionally causing unnecessary harm to another being always has an effect upon us. Harmful behavior or hurtful thinking completely wipes out trust. In its place, confusion, fear, anger, and suspicion prosper. No gain can come from doing harm to yourself, to others, or to the planet.

In order to adopt gentleness we must let go of any value we place on causing harm or upset to others—or ourselves. Even if we believe that making someone feel guilty will "teach them a lesson," we are doing harm. And, if we are being honest with ourselves, this is likely not infrequent. Whenever we choose to be negatively judgmental toward ourselves or others, we are doing harm. In essence, doing harm is any act that results from the belief that we are separate from God.

When you decide to come from a place of gentleness you are doing something very important. You are demonstrating that there is no situation, no relationship, and no event that does not occur for the purpose of deepening your awareness of Spirit.

WHEN YOU ARE GENTLE YOU STEP TOWARD GOD. WHEN YOU ARE HARMFUL YOU STEP AWAY FROM GOD.

Criticism and judgment deny us the opportunity to learn more about the power of God within. Let us commit to a new quest: to glean all that gentleness has to offer. The following excerpt from *A Course in Miracles* gives a beautiful summation on the power and impact of gentleness. Each day, before beginning the daily lessons in this section, read this to yourself:

> . . . realize that harm can actually achieve nothing. No gain can come of it. . . . who would choose the weakness that must come from harm in place of the unfailing, all-encompassing and limitless strength of gentleness?

LESSON FIVE
Let my mind be still so that I may listen to my Higher Power.

Gentleness is not complicated. It is the simplest of expressions because to be gentle is to allow God to speak through you. Gentleness comes in two steps: First, quiet your mind. Then, listen to your Higher Power. The ego has its own two-step process: Busy your mind. Listen to your fear. The outcomes are self-evident when viewed in this way. Today, make the choice to tune out the ego's voice. In exchange, tune in to the gift of gentleness from your Higher Power, which is strong in stillness and certain in its direction.

Set aside some time, preferably early in the day, to recall all of the pain and confusion that accompanies the two insane messages of the ego. No matter how loudly it shouts, recognize that the voice of the ego is not a trustworthy guide. It won't lead you to peace of mind. Ask yourself, "How can I find the peace I am looking for?"

In addition to your daily lesson, commit to taking three fifteen-minute practice periods today. During each practice, sit comfortably with your eyes closed. Deepen your breathing and begin to relax. Let go of any unwanted thoughts by focusing your attention on the smooth and rhythmic flow of your breath.

With total conviction, as you inhale say, "Let my mind be still so that I may listen to my Higher Power." Make the conscious choice to listen to your Higher Power rather than the chatter of your ego. You may not hear actual words, you may simply feel a sense of peace and relaxation. Know that God is here, patiently waiting for you to invite the power of gentleness into your life. Today, turn away from fear-based thinking. At the end of your practice period, say the following prayer and then spend some time thinking of ways you can put it into action.

Today you begin to listen to a new voice, offering a new direction grounded in gentleness. Through the Prayer for Gentleness you begin to silence all the voices that instruct you to "buy this," "control that," or "crave these" (all of which claim you are somehow deficient if you don't!). Today, you walk quietly past all of this noise with this prayer on your lips:

PRAYER FOR GENTLENESS

Dear God,

May **Your gentleness** live in all my **words**
and **actions** today.

∼ *Amen*

To each person you meet, extend a welcome hand in gentle greeting. Commit yourself to becoming a messenger of gentleness, rather than an intolerant judge. Decide to end a lifetime sentence of guilt without the possibility of parole. A kind look, a gentle glance, a soft smile rather than a preconceived opinion will reward you a thousand-fold today.

Should you find yourself in conflict in between your practice periods, be quick to turn inward and ask your Higher Power how you may use gentleness to solve the conflict. Become a joyous giver of gentleness rather than a fearful dispenser of criticism. As often as you can today, hourly would be ideal, say:

LET ME BE STILL AND LISTEN TO MY HIGHER POWER.
WHAT DOES IT MEAN TO BE TRULY GENTLE?

Then repeat the Prayer for Gentleness:

Dear God,

May Your gentleness **live** in all my words
and actions **today**.

⁓ *Amen*

Lesson Six

**Gentleness will heal the many errors
in my mind.**

Today, you enter into a state of mind no longer choked with hatred, jealousy, criticism, and revenge. This is actually the most natural of states, and it waits for you right now. Today, you do what comes naturally. Allow the state of gentleness to be as it is within you.

Unfortunately, many people run from one activity to the next—tense, stressed, without a true sense of purpose. Our culture calls this "over-achievement" or "high productivity" or just "reality."

Our culture has sold us on the idea that we need to do, or accomplish, or have, or get more of something in order to experience happiness. This is not the case. Today, we focus on the truth:

HAPPINESS IS A NATURAL RESULT OF BEING A VEHICLE FOR GOD'S GENTLENESS.

Happiness is a free-flowing stream that will run effortlessly unless dammed by fear. In other words, as long as you remain a follower of fear-based thinking, true happiness through God's gentleness will elude you. You will not find happiness through gentleness as long as you are afraid of yourself, afraid of your past, afraid of certain people, afraid of success or failure, afraid of not pleasing others, afraid of the future, afraid of disapproval, afraid of God. One action can change all of this: Once you choose to be gentle with yourself and others, your fear will diminish, and you will find, often when you least expect it, happiness has entered your life. All of this can be summed up in one sentence and is the thrust of your work today:

IF YOU WANT TO BE HAPPY, BE GENTLE.

Love, truth, and happiness are really different words describing the same thing—which is a state of mind where God's gentleness abides. God's gentleness stands in the light, out in the open. It does not hide. It is waiting for you. It is impossible to ask your Higher Power to guide you to a gentle approach to life and not find it. Today, be positive that gentleness—the fearless state of oneness with God—will enter your life. Today's lesson is geared toward achieving this state.

There is one potential obstacle: What if you think you are unworthy of the kind of gentleness being discussed here because of things you have done in the past? This is a proclamation of the ego and has no basis in truth and no business in the present moment. Know that there is no reason that gentleness and happiness are out of your reach. No matter who you are or what you may have done, you are worthy of God's love and gentleness. I invite you to consider the following meditation:

MEDITATION ON GENTLENESS

I devote this day to the decision to stop living this insane "reality" and to start living a life that is gentle and calm.

~

Begin by closing your eyes and recalling a time—even if it was less than one minute in your whole life, even if it was in a dream or in your imagination, or even if it is in a moment that is yet to come—when there was perfect stillness and peace. Envision this peaceful moment extending without limit, into eternity. Imagine this sense of stillness and gentleness can be multiplied a thousand times. This is the truth of who you are, of what God offers you, limitless in gentleness and peace. Let yourself sit and enjoy this wonderful state. Say to yourself:

This gentleness will heal all errors in my mind.

~

Continue your meditation. Build an eternal moment of gentleness by allowing the gentleness of God to flow from your mind to your family, to your workplace, to your community, to the world at large. Picture each environment—home, job, neighborhood, nation—where gentleness and forgiveness are the primary means of communication. Remind yourself that you are one with all that is and all that will be. Don't let doubt creep in. God's gentleness is a reminder of your wholeness. Remind yourself that any thoughts other than these are merely errors, illusions of the mind that are healed through gentleness. Conclude your meditation with this prayer:

Dear God,

May **Your gentleness** be in my **awareness** as I walk through my day. May my desire to be gentle **lead** me in everything that I do.

∼ Amen

If you find yourself off track during the day, simply remember to reassert your desire to follow today's lesson and say:

GENTLENESS WILL HEAL THE MANY ERRORS IN MY MIND.

Don't forget, your choice today is to be a vehicle for God's gentleness. Each time that you say, with confidence and commitment, "Gentleness will heal the many errors in my mind," you are reminding yourself that you are not separate from God. By repeating today's lesson you are affirming that gentleness will shine through any obstacle. It is with gentleness that you are able to walk through the walls of the ego.

~ JOY ~

JOY IS THE INEVITABLE RESULT OF GENTLENESS...THE OPEN
HANDS OF GENTLENESS ARE ALWAYS FILLED.

—A Course in Miracles

JOY IS WAITING FOR YOU NOW.

You are likely discovering that each of the eight traits build upon each other. For example, joy is the natural result of gentleness. With honesty, tolerance, and gentleness what could possibly interfere with joy? Joy is the outcome when we choose to follow the path of the God-centered traits of honesty, tolerance, and gentleness rather than the fear-based traits of denial, intolerance, and control.

Think of joy as an extension of gentleness based in God-centered thinking. Joy is a very simple experience, therefore it has a difficult time thriving in a busy and distracted mind. The increasingly hi-tech bounty of our culture may seem to offer opportunities for joy when in reality it more often removes us from the joyful experiences we seek. Remember:

THE ONLY THING YOU NEED TO EXPERIENCE TRUE JOY IS TO BE ALIVE IN THE MOMENT WITH SPIRIT.

Unfortunately, rather than directing our minds toward the experience of God in the present moment many of us have become numbed by too much input, stressed by too much stimulation, deadened from an overload of direct and/or indirect violence, preoccupied with financial burdens, addicted to substances, cynical about the past, and hopeless about the future. I have succumbed to all of the above from time to time. All are obstacles to joy and are precisely why I encourage you to go through each lesson in this book.

For many years my fearful mind created one obstacle after another to the joy of God. I numbed myself in every way I could imagine. As a teenager the only time I really felt "alive" was going *very* fast on my motorcycle. I tried to experience intimacy by means of drug and alcohol intoxication, thereby attaining a forced and illusory feeling of warmth and openness. Later, as an adult, I would go through the motions of enjoying a hike or a camping trip while preoccupied with work or other personal problems. I added degrees after my name, believing that academic status and prestige could be the keys to joy. The thrill-seeking behavior from adolescence continued into adulthood—this time it was aerobatic flying. I was looking for ways to feel keenly alive, to somehow overcome the distance and numbness I had created. The stakes—and risks—continued to escalate. I seemed unable to find joy in simple things. Attempting to enjoy my life was like trying to suck jello through a straw. I became very thirsty, tired, and anxious. Even after a great deal of individual therapy, dozens of self-help books, spiritual retreats, and group counseling, I still found myself looking for ways to feel joy. What I did not know is that I was longing to return home to God.

One day during a meditation I realized that if I could not experience the joy in sitting there, all the entertainment, thrill-seeking, psychotherapy, and academic honors weren't going to do me any good. In that moment I realized that joy can well up inside like a geyser. If you do not know and embrace the simplicity of *inherent internal* joy, you will find only fleeting pleasure in external pursuits. Today, I still enjoy many of the activities, but I remind myself that I bring the joy of God to *them,* rather than thinking they will bring joy to me.

WORK, PLAY, FAMILY ACTIVITIES, COMMUNITY SERVICE, AND CREATIVE PURSUITS ARE WAYS IN WHICH WE GIVE AND EXPRESS JOY, NOT WHERE WE LOOK TO FIND IT.

Think about prayer and meditation as ladles with which we dip into God's overflowing well of joy. Our activities are fueled by this joy, and each communication we have is like a cup that we gladly refill. With every expression of joy, and every cup we fill, we have more. As I write these words this is precisely what I am doing: Through prayer I have dipped my ladle into the well of God's joy, I am expressing that joy by writing, and I hope to fill a cup or two with this joy. I smile in gratitude because I receive as I give. The truth is that giving and receiving are the same.

ACCEPT THE JOY-INSPIRED LIFE GOD WANTS FOR YOU.

Joy comes from being gentle and tender in your approach to life. This requires a certain amount of sensitivity. Unfortunately, many of us were raised in ways that discouraged sensitivity and encouraged guardedness. It can be overwhelming to even consider living an unguarded life. I have faith, however, that the power of joy, gentleness, and kindness can propel us in a new direction, on both a personal and a societal level.

When we are children, there is constant pressure to learn first basic, then higher, academics and to accumulate practical skills. Few educational institutions place any emphasis on learning about one's inner self. Indeed, self-knowledge is usually left to "just happen."

PRAYER FOR JOY

Dear God,

Fill me with your joy today, and **guide my path**
with gentle and tender steps.

⁓ Amen

We can become sensitive and unguarded when we allow the daily experience of God's joy into our lives, and we do this through prayer. Sounds simple, doesn't it? But before you know it, the daily business of life seems to take priority. By practicing the daily lessons in this book you will begin to notice surprising and welcome changes in your life. Even if you should get busy and forget, try to remember this:

NO MATTER HOW LONG YOU HAVE BEEN AWAY FROM YOUR TRUE SPIRITUAL HOME, THE WALK BACK IS AS SHORT AS A SINGLE PRAYER.

Sadly, shame is often used as a way to teach "positive" lessons to children. But shame is never a good teacher. And, unfortunately, not many kids get through childhood without some of these experiences. I speak from past personal experience, and from having worked with thousands of individuals, when I tell you this. With shame we lose the ability to be sensitive to the human heart and spiritual truth. As adults we feel that we've distanced ourselves from others and God. However, experiencing the full realm of God's joy becomes impossible until shame is released.

A pessimistic scenario? Many of us, having been shamed as children, have lost the ability to be sensitive. We may even equate the words "sensitive" and "vulnerable" with pain and negative experiences. No small number of us have been criticized with the taunt, "You're too sensitive." This was me. The good news is I can personally attest that it is never too late to become spiritually sensitive. Begin by asking yourself honestly:

Do I want to acquire sensitivity to all that God offers?

It is important for you to decide what sensitivity is, and if becoming more sensitive is important to you. Study people whom you consider to be joyous. If they are hard to find, look to the great living teachers such as the Dalai Lama, or Archbishop Desmond Tutu, or the great teachers from the past, such as Jesus or the Buddha. Also observe those who seem to just exist on the planet, or seem joyless or without purpose. Isn't the difference between these two sets of people their ability or inability to be sensitive, to be gentle and tender, to dip their ladle into the well of God's joy? Notice how the joyous are able to reach out, unguarded and without fear? Whereas the lack of sensitivity deadens us while we are alive, joy brings instant renewal. Walking meditations are an excellent way to tap into the joy of the moment.

WALKING MEDITATION

Many people find it difficult to sit in meditation for extended periods of time without a lot of chatter in their minds. Walking meditation is about slowing down and finding the stillness within you, and the joy that lives in that stillness. Start out slowly at a

*pace that feels relaxed. As you walk, exhale long
and slowly. The breath will be
drawn naturally back into your body. As thoughts
arise turn your attention back to the full exhale.
Choose a quiet neighborhood or park and walk for
15-30 minutes daily.*

~

Some simple variations worth exploring:

- Walk with your hands clasped together either in front of or behind you.

- Walk with particular awareness of each foot as it touches the earth.

- Walk with your head slightly bowed.

- As you walk, imagine you are leaving a lotus flower on the ground beneath each step.

- As you walk, imagine that you are the Buddha or an enlightened being in full awareness.

- Walk with a gentle smile on your face.

- As you walk, create a rhythm by counting steps as you inhale and exhale.

Commit yourself, beginning now, to reveling in the joy

around you, and God's presence in it. Imagine that there is a volume control dial on everything around you that speaks of joy. You can turn it up whenever you want. Give the child within you the permission to explore the world and God on *your* terms. If you have children at home as I do, teach them what you want to learn. Allow them in turn to be your teachers. Take your three-year-old son or thirteen-year-old daughter for a walk, leaving a thousand thoughts about job and bills and chores at home. Look at the world through your toddler's eyes. Listen to how your teenager perceives her world. Accept them. Encourage them. Enjoy them. Believe in them.

You may encounter painful or unwanted realities in your day-to-day activities. Allow yourself to be present to what is occurring, but don't give up your sensitivity. Don't judge or label a specific event as good or bad. When you are quick to label something or someone, you remove yourself from it or them. You become a little more desensitized.

A few years ago, I saw a stray cat get hit by a car on a busy street in an affluent neighborhood during commute hour. Although I was walking a fair distance away, I noticed the driver did not stop, nor did any other cars. As I approached the injured cat, a passing pedestrian suggested, "somebody should call someone," but did not stop long enough to become involved or take responsibility. I took the cat to the vet, later caring for him at home. He was a wonderful creature, full of personality and spunk, who brought me joy and laughter.

When I reflect on that day, I see numbing effects of emotional distance. If you want joy you must be willing to react from your heart in the moment, knowing that the "cost" of caring can only be joy.

It is important to remember that being sensitive does not mean taking on another's pain, not does it mean denying their personal suffering. If you see suffering, compassionately attend to it. But there is no need to over-identify with it. This, too, turns you away from God.

In a world where there is so much suffering, becoming sensitive may seem too painful to bear. How can we find joy if all we see is suffering? Early in 1981, I had the opportunity to spend some time in India with Mother Teresa and the sisters that served with her at the Missionaries of Charity. In retrospect, I recall expecting to find the sisters depressed and "burnt out." After all, they dealt with death and disease and despair twenty-four hours a day, so I assumed the atmosphere would be bleak. What I found were the most joyful people I had ever known.

SERVING GOD IS ALWAYS A SURE PATH TO JOY.

At the Missionaries of Charity, I began to learn that being sensitive does not necessarily mean identifying with and taking on pain. Mother Teresa and the sisters were not absorbing and being overwhelmed by the suffering around them. Instead, they worked with great sensitivity, acknowledging the love, dignity, and individuality of each person in their care. This created a joy through service that transcended and transformed their efforts into devotion to God.

This experience transformed my own life because I realized that "joy through service" can come from *any* activity in *any* moment. My work, my family, and my friendships all benefit when it is my intention to serve God. I define "serving God" as any God-centered action that follows the Prayer for Joy offered on page 46.

FIND THE BEAUTY OF GOD IN EVERY MOMENT, IN ALL BEINGS, AND IN NATURE.

As I look out my window I see blue sky between the branches of oak and redwood trees. The morning sun embraces the breeze and the branches, creating shadows that dance across my desk. This lovely scene prompts the question, "What is beauty?"

I encourage you to ask yourself this question now, because beauty and joy overlap; they share common borders. Your answer may be a series of beautiful things: a fine painting, a compelling face, a child's smile, a soaring melody, or a still mountain lake. Most of us would agree that these things are beautiful. But do they define what beauty is?

It may surprise you to know that our perception of beauty, at least in part, is a learned phenomenon. We learn to judge and separate between degrees of attractiveness in people, in places and in objects, just as we learn to discriminate among such things as race, gender, and faith.

When you separate what you see into categories of appearance, or status, or even physical response—beautiful, ugly, poor, rich, pleasurable, painful—you are not likely to recognize the interconnectedness of all beings and all aspects of life. You miss the opportunity to experience joy and beauty right now. And there is no more powerful, beautiful, or joyful experience than this. The intention to be in a state of oneness with everything is the experience of beauty that leads directly to the experience of joy. It is being sensitive to all things, all aspects of life, and to God.

A house full of beautiful objects will stand empty if no love exists between the inhabitants. In the same way, it is the recognition of your connection with your Higher Power that gives meaning to external form.

I remember going into an antique shop a number of years ago where I found an elegant Japanese kimono. Because the outside was dark gray and the brightly colored lining was on the inside, I thought the storekeeper had hung it up inside out, and I brought this to his attention. In response, he smiled kindly and explained that the kimono had been made intentionally with the colorful silk on the inside to symbolize the inner beauty of the person who wore it.

Ours is a culture obsessed with physical beauty. It is ironic that in contrast to this, when you come to know your inner beauty as a reflection of God, the external world takes on an even more joyful, peaceful, and—yes—beautiful presence.

The insecure or fear-based mind does not look to the underlying oneness of life. It's too busy compensating for all those perceived fears and insecurities! From the limited and limiting perception of a fear-based mind, I may look outside my window and say that what I see is beautiful. But, from a place of being present with God, what I see deepens my joy, expands my gratitude, and heightens my awareness of love and respect for all life.

EXTEND THE LOVE GOD GIVES YOU TO EVERYONE YOU MEET.

A conversation on joy, beauty, and sensitivity would be incomplete without talking more about love. Love is not the particular domain of one religion or another; it is the thread of experience at the heart of all faiths. It is the universal experience of oneness. Love is the experience that comes from being sensitive to beauty, God, and your connection with all life.

Love does not deny any aspect of the universe. With love, we become sensitive to the animal that who is caged and the stray that is hungry, to the laughter of children walking home from school, to the tears of a friend, to the fear in the eyes of a stranger, to everything that surrounds us. This sensitivity opens the door to unconditional love and compassion. Being aware of the wholeness of our existence brings the ability to love. Without love there is only surface beauty.

When the love that exists in our hearts is shared, it has no object. This doesn't mean that you can't love another person, but it does mean that withholding love affects your capacity to experience love. The mind that loves unconditionally, or at least has this intention, sees no one as more or less worthy of love than another person. Love *is* because God *is*. It is not confined to a specific belief system or limited in any way. It comes to us when we give it.

PRAYER FOR UNCONDITIONAL LOVE

Dear God,

May I see through **Your eyes** and experience the love
for others that **You bestow upon me.**

∼ *Amen*

LESSON SEVEN
The joy and peace of God are in me now.

When we place value on fear-based thinking, we believe in guilt and shame, which become self-constructed walls against the joy and peace of God that are within us now. Today, we joyfully walk through these walls to be with the love and peace that God has kept eternally safe for us.

When we accept the idea that we are guilty ("I have done unforgivable things") and that we should be ashamed ("I am bad"), we believe we are separate from God. We fear that if the truth about us were known, we would be abandoned, even by God. Yet we rarely question this belief in our separation and shame. This false assumption creates a darkness that we dare not enter, for the demons of our past would surely overpower us.

This may sound extreme, and you may believe you really

only have the occasional guilt pang and rarely ever feel shame. Remember, even the slightest belief in guilt and shame gives power to the unforgiving thoughts that erect walls against joy. And the ego can be very effective when it comes to establishing your belief in these thoughts. Today, it is important that you see that shame and guilt are based on the past, that the past exists only in your mind, and that therefore your shame and guilt are based on *nothing* and the walls you built against joy will evaporate as you walk through them.

Today, you will begin to learn that light, joy, and peace are who you are. Today, you will learn that you are not darkness, guilt, and shame. Today, you will avoid all of those insane arguments of your ego. Today, you will focus on the truth about yourself:

THE JOY AND PEACE OF GOD ARE IN ME NOW.

The joy and peace of God have been kept safe for you throughout time. They wait for you. The fearful and shameful self that you think you created is but a bad dream. Today, you will awaken to the truth that you are one with God and all that is.

You easily walk through the wall created by shame and guilt toward the acceptance of only one thought:

YOU ARE AS THE LOVE OF GOD CREATED YOU, NOT WHAT YOU THINK YOU MADE OF YOURSELF THROUGH YOUR MISTAKES IN THE PAST.

Whatever mistakes you may have made in the past no longer have any power, unless you continue to use them to keep from being in the present moment with the joy and peace of God. This is not to say that you don't need to take responsibility for your actions and learn from your mistakes, for this is also part of the spiritual path. However, regardless of the mistakes you have made, the truth about you remains unchanged. Love is eternal and unalterable. You are, and will forever be, created in love. The joy and peace of God are in you now because they have always been there and always will be. It is that simple.

Try to devote the first five minutes of every waking hour to today's lesson. Begin by closing your eyes and briefly focusing your attention towards your breathing. Then say to yourself:

THE JOY AND PEACE OF GOD ARE IN ME NOW. IN THIS ETERNAL MOMENT I AM FREE FROM ALL MISTAKES.

Next, say:

I WILLINGLY LET GO OF ALL OF MY FALSE SELF-IMAGES.

If a thought brings you anything other than light, peace, and joy, tell yourself:

THIS THOUGHT IS NOT WHO I AM. I MADE THIS UP ABOUT MYSELF OR BELIEVED A FAULTY PERCEPTION THAT SOMEBODY ELSE TOLD ME.

Choose today to experience the unity of all that is around you. Appreciate the love of God that is present in all life. There is no need to interfere with your natural state of joy by hiding the peace of God beneath layers of shame and guilt.

You have probably had the experience of driving or walking and being so much in your thoughts that you go right past a turn or exit you need to make. Similarly, you can be so preoccupied with fear-based thoughts that you completely miss turning to the present moment, and you never arrive at the destination of the joy. Today, make the commitment to stop the mental activities of separating, labeling, judging, and categorizing—maybe even stop trying to figure everything out!

Even if you don't remember to use the first five minutes of every hour to practice, remind yourself at some point during each hour:

THE JOY AND PEACE OF GOD ARE IN ME NOW. IN THIS ETERNAL MOMENT I AM FREE FROM ALL MISTAKES.

Then take three slow and full breaths and remind yourself that this is the truth about who you are. Should a situation arise that seems to be upsetting, quickly, before giving the "upset" any fuel or power, repeat the lesson. Similarly, should anger or blame towards someone else enter into your awareness, silently address that person:

THE JOY AND PEACE OF GOD ARE IN YOU AND I NOW. IN THIS ETERNAL MOMENT YOU AND I ARE FREE FROM ALL MISTAKES.

Don't worry if you don't manage to let go of *all* guilt and shame in one day. Just know that today you start building a new foundation for living based on the joy and peace of God in the eternal moment.

LESSON EIGHT

Create a joy-inspired vision for your life.

One of the first things I do when I begin spiritual mentoring with a client is to listen for what vision they hold for their life and career. I typically don't ask by way of a direct question. Too often I'll hear a variation of the same answer: "I don't have a vision," or "I want to be successful, I just don't seem to know how," or, "A vision is a luxury, I just want to make it through the day." I try to listen to what is just beneath the reply, because this is where the fear-based vision is revealed that keeps them from a joy-inspired life.

It is important to note that two things are true as long as you are alive:

1. You breathe.

2. You have a vision.

We all have a vision because the nature of thought is: There is no such thing as a neutral thought. All thoughts create something. We all have thoughts. Thus, we all have a vision. This vision is either going to be an extension of the past, in which case it is likely to be negative, or an extension of the eternal moment, in which case it is guaranteed to be joyful. Have you invested in workshops, therapy, coaching, counseling, and self-help books, hoping they'll help you create a vision or mission statement, because you don't realize you already have one? This is a mistake, and a set-up for failure. If you paint over rust, the rust will eventually eat through the new paint. If something is rusted, your first step is to remove the rust. In the same way, if you try and place a positive vision or mission statement over a negative one that is based on a failed or painful past, the new one will be undermined and overwhelmed by the old.

Today, you are invited to begin by reminding yourself to see how valueless and limiting your old fear-based visions are: "I can't or won't succeed because I don't have enough _____ ." Just fill in the blank with your excuse of choice: money, support, encouragement, education, hair, experience, connections, and so on.

Our culture sends the message that joy comes from someplace other than in the moment with God. So it's easy to believe that joy comes from outside of ourselves. More friends, more money, or more recognition should give us more joy. Right?

Today, you will make a commitment to let go of these limiting visions and choose to devote your time to being present with the joy in the eternal moment. Paradoxically, you create a positive vision for your life when you recognize what is already here: joy. A vision for your life that is envisioned from experiencing the joy of God is driven by a power that is truly unstoppable. Today, you'll stop wasting your time focusing on negative visions from the past, stop wasting your time on just getting through the day or distracting yourself with worn out habits that don't serve you. Today, you will devote your time to experiencing the joy available to you right now.

What if I told you to look for something you had misplaced, such as your car keys, in a location that you absolutely knew was inaccurate? I doubt you would spend much energy looking there. Similarly, today's lesson is devoted to looking for a joy-inspired vision where it can be found—in the now—instead of the past, where it is not. Experience joy *right now* and create a vision for your life based on this limitless resource. Joy comes as your forgiveness begins to shine through all of the layers of darkness that you created in the form of negative visions for your life.

Celebrate yourself and the Spirit of God today. Take joy in who you are. Be thankful for the life you have and all those who come into it. They come to teach you the lessons you need to learn. When you see your life in this light, you will indeed see a can-do and joy-inspired vision.

Your exercises for today will be joyful and happy ones. You will extend gratitude for the passing of the old limiting visions. You will begin with forgiveness as you let go of the negative past. Remind yourself that forgiveness is your sole purpose for today. Forgiveness is the "celestial rust remover" that will allow your new vision to come through unmarred by the past. Know that there is no more important task than this. Your singleness of purpose will make your goal reachable. Begin your practice periods by telling yourself:

HOLDING ONTO A PAINFUL PAST IS HOW I CREATE A NEGATIVE VISION FOR MY FUTURE. A JOY-INSPIRED VISION AWAITS ME IN THE ETERNAL PRESENT MOMENT. FORGIVENESS IS HOW I ARRIVE IN THE ETERNAL PRESENT MOMENT.

Do not dwell on the past today. Instead, practice forgiveness. Let your Higher Power wash your mind of all the limiting ideas that you thought were true. Pray to free yourself from all the negative perceptions you have made about yourself. Today, meet yourself as though for the first time. Wait for who you are in the silence of the present moment. As you wait, slowly repeat the following prayer:

Dear God,

I humbly ask **Your help** in forgiving myself and
all people in my life. May the light of **Your joy** illuminate
Your vision for my life, and may I trust
in **Your strength** now and always.

∾ Amen

Your shorter practice periods are simply momentary reminders of your goal for the day. Remember that today is a time of celebration in which you give thanks for life itself and take joy in the power of forgiveness. Know with confidence that today marks a new beginning for you. A new, joy-inspired vision is being born.

Before going to bed, remember: This day was dedicated to the serenity that is with you at all times. It marks a beginning in that you are forgiving yourself as your positive vision is revealed and replaces the guilt and shame that you once thought were real. Joy is in you, and it can now be manifest and shared with others. Extend forgiveness to yourself and others and you will never be without joy. As you go to sleep let your dreams celebrate the beginning of your new vision that has come to you today.

~ DEFENSELESSNESS ~

THE GENTLE LETTING GO OF THE DEMANDS AND ATTACH-
MENTS OF YOUR MIND REPRESENTS THE HIGHEST LEVEL OF
TRUE STRENGTH AND CHARACTER IN A HUMAN BEING.

—Ken Keyes, Jr., *Prescriptions for Happiness*

**DEFENSELESSNESS IS TO BE WITHOUT JUDGMENT, NEI-
THER AFRAID NOR PREDICTING ATTACK BY OTHERS.**

Defenselessness is the most natural thing in the world. It is a
direct reflection and acknowledgment of someone who has
chosen to trust their Higher Power. To be defenseless does not
mean that you throw yourself into dangerous circumstances
with reckless abandon. Rather, to be defenseless means in the
present moment you choose to turn your life over to the direction of your Higher Power, rather than blindly defending your
unexamined attachments. One of the great paradoxes you will

encounter on your spiritual journey is that to create a future that is limitless in possibility you need to let go of your attachments as to how you think things should unfold.

OUR ATTACHMENTS GET IN THE WAY OF THE GIFTS GOD TRIES TO BRING TO US.

While we are busy trying to make happen what we think *should* happen, we overlook the opportunities that our Higher Power presents. Unfortunately, we don't just miss opportunities when we are glued to our attachments. The ego creates further havoc because it believes that whatever is valuable to us (i.e., our attachments) must be defended. In fact, I believe most personal conflicts are a result of this belief. Unwavering peace of mind comes when we fully realize we are the essence of God's love. Love is the one thing that needs no defense. Indeed, our defenses actually hide love from us.

This principle is acceptable, even obvious, once the belief system of fear-based thinking is seen for what it is: an ideology based on fear that is rooted in the past.

When I was a child growing up in Tiburon, in Northern California, an old man lived above a ramshackle storefront in the town center. Peeking into the dust-caked windows of the shop below his apartment revealed stacks of pans and baking implements, and a barely visible sign that proclaimed Morreli's Bakery.

Mr. Morreli cut a short, stocky figure and was rarely seen without his cigar, when he was seen at all. He ran the bakery by himself, although it was seldom open for business. This reclusive man kept the drapes to his upstairs apartment drawn and the doors to his bakeshop shut and locked.

The old man's life puzzled me. Was he lonely? And why would anyone own a store that almost never opened? Such questions stayed with me even as I grew older and eventually left my parents' home and moved away.

When I finished college I moved back to my hometown. I was pleasantly surprised to hear that Mr. Morreli was still living. He had moved his always-closed bakery to a smaller location, but retained the apartment upstairs. I often thought of Mr. Morreli and wondered what his life was like.

At the time, in the mid 1970s, I happened to be renting a house from a man named John who regularly visited Mr. Morreli. John gave the elderly baker a great deal of loving support. I was touched by their relationship and John's commitment to help Mr. Morreli's life close in a dignified manner.

In recent years, Mr. Morreli's memory has served as a metaphor, reminding me of the foolish ways I have guarded and defended myself: How many times have I noticed myself harboring a belief system that was rarely open? A heart that was bolted shut? A mind full of useless attachments I insisted were precious? And a house full of possessions I believed I couldn't live without?

It has been a long time now since I lived in Tiburon, and many years since Mr. Morreli passed away. Yet I still see traces of Morreli's Bakery in the windows that now house a trendy boutique.

When I look up to the windows that once revealed tired yellowing drapes, I remind myself of the importance to open my heart to God in each and every moment.

When we are defensive it is because we believe: a) we have something that we are attached to—a thought, an idea, a possession, a person—that we believe needs defending, and b) our defenses will make us safe. One of the most important lessons we will ever learned is: It is not danger that comes when we lay down our defenses. It is safety. It is peace of mind. It is joy.

No matter how strong a violent storm, a mountain does not need to defend itself from it. The mountain knows its strength. On your spiritual path you will come to realize that what has value needs no defense because you know your strength is with God. Love, compassion, kindness, tolerance, truth, honesty, gentleness, joy generosity, patience...these need no defense—ever. This is because they reflect God and what is of God needs no defense. As your trust in God grows, you will become less defensive naturally.

I once had a Queensland Heeler named Vali who was quite intelligent but also very protective to the degree that she had a hard time having fun when other dogs came to visit. I remember one occasion when some friends brought their dogs over to the house. The two visitors played together for hours, rolling in the grass and chasing one another. Vali, on the other hand, was either guarding her bed or protecting her food dish throughout the afternoon and never joined in the fun.

When I am honest with myself, I can see that over the

years at various times I have behaved a lot like Vali. Whenever I have chosen to be defensive instead of defenseless I have been just like her, on guard instead of in the moment and enjoying it. It is important to recognize the thought system that lies beneath a defensive attitude and behavior. I have found four consistent barriers to defenselessness:

1. Unexamined attachments and fear of loss makes us defensive and guarded.

2. We are defensive when we protect something that is ego-based and valueless.

3. We become reactively defensive when we don't see the opportunities God is bringing us in the moment that is here now.

4. We are defensive when we think it is important to be right.

Consider a child who wants to have things his way, is presented with something that is going to be great fun, but throws a tantrum over what he will have to "give up" in exchange for the fun. He can't see the opportunity because he wants what he wants. Our adult defenses are no less faulty, they just become more sly and manipulative. However, once our defenses are seen for what they are, we realize they are little more than the immature part of our mind acting out. I can say this because I have known the agony and isolation that defensiveness has brought to me.

It is not difficult to see that defensiveness is fear-based, short-sighted, and costs us dearly. The ego is always at the core of defensiveness, whereas our Higher Power is always at the core of openness—letting go of attachments that get in the way of seeing the opportunities God brings us everyday.

- ❧ Without excessive attachments we no longer feel in need of defense.

- ❧ Without defenses we can find the peace of God in the present moment.

- ❧ With the help of our Higher Power, our attachments and defenses are released and replaced with traits offered by God.

PRAYER FOR
RELEASE OF ATTACHMENTS AND DEFENSES

Dear God,

Help me to **release** my attachments to all that does not bring me peace. **Help me** to lay down my defenses so that I find **Your peace** in this moment.

∼ *Amen*

WHEN I CHANGE MY MIND I CHANGE MY LIFE.

Throughout this book I have said and will continue to say that fear and upset will prevent you from being able to listen to your Higher Power. I repeat it so much because I believe it to be true. Don't make the mistake of believing that you are only responsible for what you do, but not for what you think. We are each responsible for what we think, and it is our thinking that makes us do the things we do—good and bad. This is great news because our thoughts are within our control to change, whereas most external circumstances are not. Behavior follows thought. Remember this and you are automatically on the right track.

There is nothing more singularly powerful than reclaiming and developing the power of thought. Whether under our conscious direction or not, our thoughts create every minute of every day. Behavior is a symptom of an underlying thought. As such, any approach or path to growth that only changes behavior is incomplete. It is true that behavioral change can occur by reinforcement or punishment without ever addressing the thought or subjective experience that is beneath. In some cases, quite profound behavioral change can be made in this way. However, this does not speak to the individual's inner subjective experience, and the behavior change is usually short-lived.

If peace of mind is your goal, you must change your mind, not just your behavior. This most definitely requires a willingness to become more defenseless, and a desire to experience the peace of God. Defensiveness is always a sign that you believe you are separate from others and from God. Belief in separation usually incites belief in the need to defend. Conversely, whenever there is the recognition of your underlying oneness with God, there is peace of mind through defenselessness.

You become defensive when you have not made up your mind about who you are and what you want. The ego functions in split goals, and the result is always conflict. With two opposing thoughts, even when one is potentially positive, the mind is caught in a type of double-bind. I may be certain, for example, that a positive goal is to develop relationships with people who are supportive of me and see my potential. Yet, if I also secretly hold the belief that I am undeserving because of things I have done in the past, I will not be happy when I receive their support.

Remember, only your mind can produce an upset, and only your mind can resolve it. One way your mind creates an upset is by having a potentially positive goal, and then making it impossible to achieve because of a conflicting goal or belief. The sabotaging thoughts of old fear-based thinking can be remedied by accepting the unifying goal of God-centered thinking. What follows are some examples of positive goals followed by conflicting beliefs:

- I want to be self-confident.

- But if people see who I really am I will not be accepted.

- To be a good person I need strong moral values.

- But I have done things that are unforgivable.

- I want to love and be loved.

- But I should beware of being hurt at all times.

- I want to feel close to other people and God.

- But to be safe I should judge others and be sure not to miss anything.

- I want to be happy.

- But I need the approval of others.

The following are some examples of unifying goals that promote God-centered thinking:

MY GOAL IS TO ACCEPT RATHER THAN JUDGE OTHERS.

Dear God,

Help me to overcome my judgments and **accept** what **You** bring me to learn from.

~ *Amen*

MY GOAL IS TO RELEASE MYSELF FROM THE BONDAGE OF THE PAST.

Dear God,

Release me from the bondage of the past I think is real and show me **Your love** in this moment.

~ *Amen*

MY GOAL IS TO FOCUS ON HEALING RATHER THAN HURTING.

Dear God,

Guide me to be a vehicle for healing, and **help me** to see that causing harm will never bring me anything I want.

∼ *Amen*

MY GOAL IS TO FORGIVE MYSELF AND OTHERS.

Dear God,

Let me always **see forgiveness** as **the answer**.

∼ *Amen*

MY GOAL IS TO KNOW ALL THAT LOVE OFFERS AND TO DO THIS BY OFFERING LOVE.

Dear God,

Reveal to me Your love, and **make me a vehicle** to bring it to others.

∼ *Amen*

I WILL NEVER FIND CONSISTENT PEACE IF I HAVE NOT
MADE UP MY MIND ABOUT WHO I AM AND WHAT I WANT.

When we become defensive we have accepted a fear-based reality that tells us we are in constant danger. If we do not question the foundation that our defensiveness and fear rest on, we will never find peace of mind. In fact, we will continue to build elaborate defenses believing this will create a safe existence.

To move beyond defensiveness, we need only remember that love is our natural inheritance and the truth about who we are. God's love never abandons us. We abandon God and His love when we hide it under layers of guilt, judgment, and shame. Once hidden, we can choose to believe that love has disappeared and that guilt and shame are who we are.

What every human being wants is to experience love, kindness, and union with other people and God. Beyond all other goals and achievements we may have, and regardless if we are fully aware of it or not, this yearning is in our hearts and minds when we arrive into this world and when we depart from it.

You may look around you and see a world that demands defenses for survival. However, there is another way of looking at the world. Recall that regardless of what their behavior may be, what people are really asking for is love. So, despite all that we say and do, there are only two forms of communication:

- Extending love.

- Making a call for love.

Unfortunately, most "calls for love" rarely look like what they are. More typically, when someone acts in anger, with dishonesty, or goes on the attack, the thought, "this person is making a call for love, let me respond to this" is usually not the first thought to cross your mind. Yet, I suggest that each and every time, such displays of bad temper or behavior are, at their core, a call for love and understanding.

Earlier in my career as a psychologist, I spent quite a bit of time with troubled teenagers, and in them I have seen some very elaborate defense systems. The increase in teen suicide and pregnancy, as well as unsafe schools, drug use, and gang activity are just a few examples. I found that most every single defensive behavior was a call for love, understanding, and compassion. This, of course, did not mean that no boundaries were set, or all I did was to sit and tell them I loved them. But without this awareness my intervention would have been lacking. I asked myself what these young people believed about themselves and the world to cause their isolating, self-destructive, and dishonest behavior. To be of any help at all, I had to be willing to explore with them their inner subjective lives—which they kept so well guarded—and I needed to do it with love, caring, and compassion.

Loving and compassionate responses have become rare in our culture as we teach our children to adopt fear-based attitudes. In today's often frightening and increasingly violent world, this is sometimes difficult to argue against. However, although precautions are necessary and wise, it is also necessary and wise to embrace the understanding that we are safe and secure in God's love.

When I was still in practice as a psychologist, Paul and Carol Applegate came to see me. They were concerned and confused about their son Rick, a troubled sixteen-year-old. Rick had been caught using marijuana and lying about skipping school. Before five minutes of our session had elapsed, I realized Paul and Carol were in a great deal of emotional pain, which revealed itself in several ways.

Paul, a tall man with slightly graying hair, appeared mildly out of place in his business suit. I wondered if he wore it to the session to reassure himself of his own authority, as he clearly felt none with his son. Carol sat sobbing as her husband distantly and matter-of-factly told me of their problems with Rick. The more Paul spoke, the deeper Carol sunk into her chair, as though she wanted to disappear into the pattern of the fabric. There was nothing accusatory in Paul's tone of voice—indeed it resembled a newscaster recounting yet another tragedy—but it was clear that they both believed Carol was to blame for Rick's behavior. Apparently, they thought that someone had to be blamed. Possessing little self-esteem, Carol covertly volunteered, as she probably had for many things in her life.

As the session continued, a picture of their son Rick began to emerge. Apparently the young man had been well-behaved and a model student until entering high school. An only child, Rick served as the center of Carol's life for many years. With adolescence, however, he began distancing himself from her. To Carol it was as though she were losing her only companion.

Due to a combination of professional responsibilities and a desire to avoid the problems at home, Rick's father was away a great deal of the time. (Avoidance, often by "staying busy," is a common way for an individual to stay troubled.) In fact, Paul spent less and less time with his family as the years went on. During our session, he repeatedly emphasized his responsibilities to the family; for him, responsibilities meant that he had to make a certain amount of money. And although Paul plainly loved his son, he did so from such emotional distance that Rick never knew it.

Paul was not sure how, or where, or when to begin dealing with Rick's current problems and showed no emotion whatsoever during our first session. In the second session, however, Paul became angry when he described how his son defied his "orders." (One way to avoid dealing with anger is to become internally numb or emotionally flat. This eventually causes either "implosion," which results in emotional stress and physical problems, or "explosion," which usually results in damaged relationships.)

Rick had been experimenting with marijuana, though it did not yet appear that he was chemically dependent. Although neither parent consumed alcohol or other drugs, Paul had grown up in an alcoholic home. Also, neither Paul nor Carol were able to communicate much about their feelings, even though both were clearly in emotional pain. (Denial of pain and problems as a way of dealing with them leads to poor communication.)

It was clear to me after a few sessions that Rick was acting out in a variety of ways that reflected issues in the family. Both parents seemed surprised when I suggested family counseling, and seemed to conclude this meant they had been "bad" parents. They would have preferred it if I had asked them to bring Rick in to be "fixed," then returned him as soon as he was "back to normal."

I explained to them that families work as a system (as do all groups), and that one member will often manifest the problems that underlie a "system" conflict. For change to occur, every member must participate. In this particular family, the first obstacle to overcome was the belief that there had to be someone to blame. With family therapy, the emphasis would be on growth, not fault.

Initially, Rick was a reluctant participant in therapy. Time spent with his parents usually meant time spent being criticized. As time went on, he was able to talk about his real feelings—anger, pain, fear, and frustration—rather than continuing his defensive and distancing behavior. Though his parents loved Rick very much, they had problems communicating their feelings to him. Paul was critical and controlling, and rarely expressed his love in positive ways. Carol, who tended to feel powerless, seldom offered any limits or direction.

As therapy progressed it became clear that Paul felt competent and confident at work, but inadequate and awkward in his role as a father. Not surprisingly, he placed a higher priority on his career, where he felt more successful, which further distanced him from his son. Not surprisingly, Rick felt that his father didn't really like him. Unable to speak about how much this hurt him, Rick began to act out. Slowly they were both able to let their feelings be known and, as time went on, they were able to be more present and genuine with one another, both during the sessions and at home.

Carol and Paul had never given much thought to their relationship as a couple, but simply continued on the familiar "tread mill" of marriage. With therapy, they were able to get beyond blame and explore themselves and each other. This also had an effect on Rick, for he had never really seen his parents relate on an emotional level. Up to then, he had had no role models for how to effectively communicate feelings.

Carol became more assertive in her relationship with her husband, and with her son. Rick previously had little respect for his mother. Because he had seen so many people treat her poorly, including Paul, Rick did so too. Indeed, he would rage at his mother at the drop of a hat. (Being a victim creates being a victim.) With time, Rick learned how to discuss his feelings, and so became better able to reveal his anger in an effective, rather than a hurtful or destructive way.

Each family member had been defensive in their thinking and behavior, though previously only Rick's behavior had stood out. Each person needed to identify and work through his or her own fears and defenses. Most importantly, each stopped responding negatively to defenses and was able to find what was really needed: a spiritual focus with practical changes.

- ❧ Stop denying problems and pain.

- ❧ Rather than avoiding uncomfortable situations, be honest and open to finding healing solutions.

- ❧ Rather than blaming negative behavior, model positive behavior.

- ❧ Acknowledge anger, but release it through forgiveness.

- ❧ Give up being a victim and see the power to change within you.

I COMMIT TO WANTING SOMETHING DIFFERENT THAN THAT WHICH MY DEFENSIVENESS BRINGS ME AND RE-PLACING IT WITH A GOD-CENTERED EXPERIENCE.

Five Steps to Reduce Defensive Behavior

1. **Identify the defensive behavior you are engaging in.** Is your behavior pushing people or God away? Is your behavior motivated by fear, upset, or anger?

   Dear God,

   Help me to see the ways in which I think I push You
   and the people You have sent to me away.

   ∼ *Amen*

2. **Identify the thought or belief that is behind your defensive behavior.** Remember that every behavior is preceded by a belief or assumption. Fear-based beliefs always lead to defensive behavior and feelings of isolation. To find the thought behind your defensive behavior, ask yourself: "How and why am I feeling unsafe?" "What am I holding on to from the past that is making me feel hurt and/or angry?" "What judgments am I holding?"

Dear God,

Help me to see the ways in which I think
I push You and the people You have sent
to me away.

〜 *Amen*

3. **Identify what it is that you really want.** Ultimately, this will always be an aspect of experiencing the love of God in the moment.

Dear God,

Show me what it is that **You** would have me
want so that I may find Your love and peace
that is **always** here.

〜 *Amen*

4. **Identify what you can do to create what you want,** rather than continuing to act defensively. Ask yourself:

"What behavior would demonstrate my commitment to forgiveness?" "How could I give what it is I want to receive?" "If my peace of mind is my single goal, right now, how do I want to act?"

Dear God,

Show me what it is that **You** would have me do to find
Your love and peace that is **always** here.

⌒ Amen

5. **Identify the God-centered belief or attitude that would lead to this behavior.** This will always include knowing the love of God is in you now. Also, remind yourself that all forms of communication either extend love or are calls for love.

Dear God,

Show me what it is that **You** would have me believe
in order to find Your love and peace
that is **always** here.

⌒ Amen

Not long ago, as the holiday season approached, I was feeling a bit gloomy. Although I enjoy the holidays, I come from a divorced home and am divorced myself, and sometimes this creates a sadness in me, a longing that never quite seems to be filled, even though all parties are now very good friends. This particular Thanksgiving I noticed old feelings of loneliness resurfacing. I also found myself being short-tempered and somewhat withdrawn from my kids, which is unusual for me. This defensive behavior needed to be addressed so that I could get to where I wanted to be: happy and present throughout the season. I utilized the five steps to reduce defensive behavior and, despite having practiced them many times before, it still took some serious reflection and prayer to complete. Below I share a simplified version of my process with you:

1. **Identify the defensive behavior.**
   How am I pushing God and the people He sent to me away?
   I am being short, isolating myself, and acting from an old tension in my gut.

2. **Identify the thought or belief behind the defensive behavior.**
   How and why am I feeling unsafe?
   I am turning to the painful past rather than to my Higher Power at this moment.
   What am I holding on to from the past that is making me feel hurt and angry?
   I am holding on to the times I believed I was abandoned, when I felt alone.
   What judgments am I holding?
   Other people are not here for me and this is what the future holds.

What am I thinking that pushes God and the people He
sent to me away?

I believe I am alone and separate from God and other
people.

3. **Identify what it is I really want.**

What is it that God would have me want to find His love
and peace that is always here?

I want to give and receive love right now in this moment.

4. **Identify what I can do to create what I want, instead
of continuing to act defensively.**

What behavior would demonstrate my commitment to
forgiveness?

I need to show up, be in the present moment, and reach
out to people.

How can I give what I want to receive?

I can extend love and thoughts of gratitude.

If peace of mind is my goal, right now, how do I want to
act?

I want to act with serenity and trust in God.

What is it that God would have me do to find His love
and peace that is always here?

Give to others what He offers me right now.

5. **Identify the beliefs or attitudes that lead to this behavior.**

What it is that God would have me think in order to find
His love and peace that is always here?

I do not have to worry about what to do, how to act, or what to say because God will express His love through me right now.

LESSON NINE
Letting go of comparisons is the way to gratitude.

Today, you begin living in gratitude for the one force that heals all suffering: God's love. For example, when you are aware of those less fortunate than you, be grateful that you can extend compassion, kindness, and prayer to them, perhaps even do something to help with their condition. Or, when you see those who seem to have more than you, be happy for their good fortune rather than envious. If you can't stop comparing, then for now focus on changing your response to what you see.

Two sure-fire ways to set your life on a disastrous course are to compare and then:

- ❧ Be envious of those who have good fortune.

- ❧ Ignore those less fortunate, or use them to make yourself feel lucky.

Two sure-fire ways to set your life on a positive course are to:

- ❧ Be happy for those who have good fortune.

- ❧ Help someone who is in need.

Remember, our attitudes come from our beliefs. When we forget we are completely loved by God, and believe we are separate from God, we adopt the negative attitudes of guardedness, defensiveness, scarcity, and condemnation. These attitudes are self-defeating and self-perpetuating.

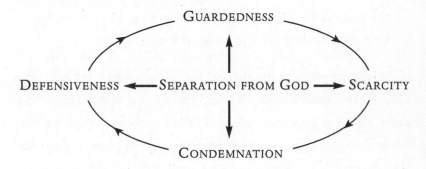

When we remember that we are loved by God, we adopt the positive attitudes of openness, defenselessness, abundance, and kindness. These are also self-perpetuating.

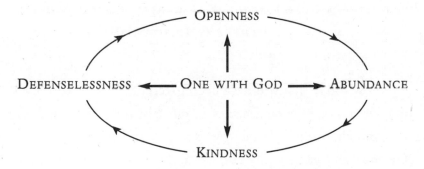

A positive attitude, such as gratitude, is impossible to adopt when we believe we are victims or when we make constant comparisons, and a posture of rigid defensiveness will surely follow. Instead, commit to seeing the lessons of love and compassion everywhere and in everything—even in situations that you don't like or don't see an immediate purpose for. You won't have to "try" to be grateful, your gratitude will simply grow.

LOVE MAKES NO COMPARISONS, AND EXCLUDES NO ONE. TODAY I COMMIT TO THE PRACTICE OF LOVE.

Seeing ourselves as spiritual beings, not separate from others or God, creates gratitude for each and every living thing. This is how defenselessness comes into being. All the comparisons between ourselves and others have done nothing but delay the peace and serenity that are available to us at all times. Remember that hatred, jealousy, and resentment do not exist when comparisons are laid aside.

TODAY, I PLEDGE TO LAY COMPARISONS ASIDE. INSTEAD, I CHOOSE TO EXTEND LOVE AND COMPASSION. I AM GRATEFUL I CAN DO THIS, I AM GRATEFUL EACH TIME I DO IT, AND I KNOW THERE IS NO SITUATION IN WHICH THIS CANNOT BE DONE.

Know today that you have been given everything you need in order to experience peace of mind right now. You can deny this and choose to give energy to anger, malice, and revenge. Or you can just as easily choose to have gratitude for God's love and allow it to replace those insane perceptions. Thus, when you are tempted to fall back on comparisons, remember:

THERE IS ANOTHER CHOICE. I CHOOSE GRATITUDE.

Gratitude and love occupy the same mind, and build upon each other. Similarly, anger, jealousy, hatred, envy, and fear can also crowd your thoughts, and they, too, build upon each other. Gratitude is an aspect of love. It is a doorway that allows abundance to enter and defensiveness to leave. Today, remind yourself many times:

LETTING GO OF COMPARISONS IS THE WAY TO TRUE GRATITUDE.

Lesson Ten
Look to yourself for gratitude.

Have you become accustomed to looking to other people for gratification, gratitude, and validation? Do you attempt to be compassionate, kind, and forgiving, but stop if you don't get validation from others? You may find yourself returning to your old fear-based ways when you don't get the responses you expect.

NOW IT IS TIME TO UNDERSTAND THAT IT IS ONLY YOUR GRATITUDE AND GOD'S THAT MATTER.

Looking to others for validation is just the ego talking and originates in the belief that your happiness is dependent on outside approval of others.

GOD IS GRATEFUL FOR EVERY LOVING THOUGHT AND
COMPASSIONATE ACTION THAT YOU BRING TO THE WORLD.

Today, be concerned with who you are right now, not what
you have or have not done in the past. You may find it helpful
to begin by being grateful for your capacity to be kind to
another living being. Is this not a precious and beautiful gift
that is always available to you? Make the following commitment, each and every hour of the day:

NO MATTER WHAT HAPPENS, TODAY MY EMPHASIS IS ON
BEING KIND TO PEOPLE, IN BOTH THOUGHT AND ACTION.

Allow your kindness to expand to all the people in your life.
Even those with whom you are most tempted to become
defensive are here to teach you how to choose another way of
thinking, acting, and being.

WHEN YOU ARE DEFENSIVE AND AFRAID, YOU HAVE NOTH-
ING. WHEN YOU ARE KIND WITH A GRATEFUL HEART, YOU
HAVE EVERYTHING.

You may assume that a lack of obvious positive response to
your gifts of compassion and gratitude means the gifts were
not received or have gone unrecognized. If the recipient's
behavior does not change, you may conclude your efforts were
ignored. At such times you may be tempted to revert back to
anger, attack, resentment, and defense. Remember that it does
not matter whether or not your gifts are considered worthy.
Remind yourself often:

I KNOW THAT NO KIND OR LOVING THOUGHT GOES
UNNOTICED.

Through the years I worked with some very angry and defensive people—gang members, inmates, addicts, abuse survivors—and I sometimes thought I was not reaching them. On several occasions I have encountered these people years later and some have said, "Hey, Doc, you know I never thanked you for those times you talked with me. Thanks." Translation: "Thanks for the love and kindness when I needed it most, even though I was too afraid and guarded to let it show back then." I have learned to never, ever, underestimate the power of love and kindness, and for this I am grateful. I trust that no loving thought goes unnoticed, even when I do not see immediate gratitude or behavior changes in the other person.

Even with those you love—friends, spouse, parents, children—there are probably times when it is tempting to withdraw your kindness when their appreciation is not obvious and blame them or make them feel guilty for being ungrateful or unappreciative. Today, make the commitment to not do this, for such behavior never gives anyone peace. Be kind and trust that your gift is received and makes a difference.

The focus of today's lesson is simply this: Be grateful for your capacity to be kind and loving. Gratitude is a part of love, and the experience of love is all that your Higher Power is concerned with.

Dear God,

Help me to extend kindness, and be **thankful**
my heart is full.

Forgive, and be **grateful** that I am forgiven.

Love, and receive my gift as I **give** it.

Have gratitude, and know I am **complete.**

~ *Amen*

~ GENEROSITY ~

EVEN IF YOU KNEW A THOUSAND TIMES MORE OF YOURSELF, YOU WOULD NEVER REACH BOTTOM. YOU WOULD STILL REMAIN AN ENIGMA TO YOURSELF, AS YOUR FELLOW MAN WOULD REMAIN AN ENIGMA TO YOU. THE ONLY WAY TO FULL KNOWLEDGE LIES IN THE ACT OF LOVE; THIS ACT TRANSCENDS THOUGHT, IT TRANSCENDS WORDS.

—Erich Fromm, *The Art of Loving*

Many of us learn that the world is a place where there is not enough to go around, where you work hard to get what you have, and then guard what you have acquired. With such a belief in place, an act of generosity is based on and equated with the sense of losing something. To the ego, giving anything away is equated with having less. Who would opt to do so? With such a perspective, we can only be "generous" when we know what is in it for us. Generosity becomes little more than a calculation of what we will lose and what we might get in return: a cost-benefit analysis. There is a better way.

To know the difference between authentic, abundance-based generosity and false, fear-based generosity is to know the difference between giving from the ego and giving from the heart.

Authentic generosity is an attitude based on abundance, the knowledge that we have all we need. Whereas generosity based on scarcity calculates potential losses and payoffs. Generosity based on abundance gives away in order to keep. Remember:

All that is of God only increases as you give it away.

Not only does this principle hold true for compassion and love, tolerance and kindness, abundance-based acts of generosity open the doors to the natural flow of all forms of wealth. What makes this concept tricky to grasp? It may be because it represents a reversal of the message we get about wealth from our culture. Fear-based thinking creates scarcity-based generosity, whereas God-centered thinking creates abundance-based generosity. The difference is literally night and day—one will bring darkness and the other light. The path you follow determines the level of abundance in your life. The importance of this cannot be stressed enough.

Scarcity-based generosity relies on camparing, competing, and, above all else, withholding:

1. Compare how much you have and how much others have. Give something away only if you can "afford" it. In order to afford to be generous you must constantly acquire, hoard, and skimp.

2. Only do so if you can either look good doing it or get something in return.

3. Use generosity as a tool for manipulation. If you give, have a clear idea of what you will get in return, when you will get it, and consider consequences if you don't.

4. Be aware that there is never enough of what you need. Always raise your requirements when you get what you previously thought was enough.

5. If someone else has more, try to catch up or surpass them. Power comes from having more than others.

6. Never be generous with someone you don't like or who has "done you wrong."

7. Don't be "too" generous because then other people will expect more from you in the future.

Abundance-based generosity requires nothing except to give away as much as you can:

1. Lay comparisons aside. That which is of value grows more so as you give it away.

2. Giving, without attachment or expectations, guarantees peace and prosperity.

3. Give for the sake of giving, because this is how you in turn will receive.

4. There is an endless supply of what you want. So there is no need to keep score.

5. To be generous you need do nothing other than recognize the truth about who you are.

6. Generosity is not just a single act, but is an attitude. To have a generous spirit is to mirror God.

7. Withholding generosity from another is the same as withholding it from yourself.

LOOK TO THOSE WHO "LIVE TO GIVE" AND FOLLOW THEIR EXAMPLE.

During the past thirty years I have witnessed poverty and suffering on the streets of Bombay, in Cambodian refugee camps, and in homeless shelters and mental health clinics in the United States. I have seen the anguish of many, but I have also watched miracles unfold. It is not that death, disease, mental illness, addiction, and starvation don't exist—it is the unconditional love and generosity of the people who give of themselves in these devastating circumstances that vanquish fear and replace it with peace. Regardless of its "size," each act of generosity helps to transform despair into hope and degradation into dignity.

Believing I was powerless to do anything positive when I was first confronted by suffering, I recall the gnawing feeling in my gut, part of me wanted to run. But over the years I have found that the decision to give from a place of generosity, knowing that each act has a singular and cumulative effect on us and on those to whom we give—no matter how small the gesture may appear—does make a difference. So rather than seeing myself as separate from other people, and powerless to act, I seek to understand others, and focus on my ability to give. I may not be able to end starvation, but I can extend love, prayer, and compassion through action. This most certainly makes a difference—to myself, to other individuals, and to the world.

The same love that created you created me, and created the person who suffers. When confronted with suffering, or any challenge in life, we must remember to direct our consciousness to the love that bonds us to one another. The gift of love is available to us at all times, and it is a gift to be shared, a gift we must use.

Many of us, including myself, ask, "What is our purpose?" There are many books written on this subject. Isn't the answer fairly straightforward? Isn't it to help each other know love through compassionate action? I believe we are here to give and receive love. *And it is not how much we give but how much love we put into the giving that matters.* My life purpose has become that simple.

It is not likely that you and I will be generous in action and spirit all the time. We are, after all, only human. What is important is that we have *intention*—that we *want* to give love, that we *want* to be generous, that we *want* to listen, that we *want* to give whatever it takes with joy. When I wake up in the morning I try to remind myself that, whatever happens on that day, *this* is my intention. I might not be perfect at it, but even a moment or two of generosity can make a huge difference in my life and the lives of those around me.

In my own experience, I have learned about generosity in many places, from many people. Earlier I mentioned I had the rare opportunity of spending time with Mother Teresa in India. I felt blessed to be in her presence and took the opportunity to ask her a variety of questions that were important to me. Somehow, all her answers revealed the core principles of generosity, even when she was not speaking literally or directly about giving.

YESTERDAY IS GONE. TOMORROW HAS NOT YET COME. AND SO WE HAVE ONLY TODAY TO MAKE SOMETHING BEAUTIFUL FOR GOD.

Through the years, I have found it extremely helpful to return to her words. What follows is a list of her wisdom that I have read and reread time and time again. Sometimes, I need to read the whole list to myself several times, until the world and my life begin to make sense again. At other times, I will choose one or two lines to apply throughout the day.

The Wisdom of Mother Teresa

- Listen from the silence of your heart, speak from the fullness of your heart.

- The joy of loving is always between two. It begins with two, and grows from there.

- We have only today to make something beautiful for God.

- If we have a clean heart we can see, we can understand, and we can accept each other in the gift of love.

- The same love that created you also created me.

- We must bring our life to a oneness with the love that abounds within us. And to be able to do this we need a clean heart.

- We all have the gift of love and it is a gift to be shared.

- Love is a gift and we must use it to increase love and compassion.

- We must give up our desire to destroy.

- We must begin to help each other.

- We must transform love beyond words and show it through our actions.

- Our purpose is to help each other to know, to hear, and to love.

- We are here to exchange the means and ways of love.

- Let us put love into action.

- Let us know love begins at home.

- Let us bring back love and generosity into our lives, into our families.

- There is no greater science than the science of love.

- It is not how much you give but how much love you put into the giving.

- Maybe in our own home we can begin, maybe today. Maybe somebody there needs our love.

- Let us keep the joy of loving going in our heart.

- Share your joy with all beings, especially people at home with you.

- Come home.

- Those close to you need your love.

- Our children need our tenderness, appreciation, and gentle embrace.

- We don't need bombs and other defenses in order to bring peace. We need tender love and compassion and the sharing of joy that comes naturally from loving one another.

- We must want to give whatever it takes with joy.

- You are precious and you are loved tenderly.

- We must respect all that we do in understanding love.

- If we really understand love, we are ready to give that love.

- The demonstration that we understand love is that we share love with everyone.

- If it doesn't penetrate the heart, if it is not coming from the heart to the heart, we can do very little to fully understand love.

- Something that comes from one heart to another heart will remain there, because it is in the silence of the heart that God speaks.

- It is from the fullness of the heart that we may fully give and receive.

- Listening is the beginning.

- Listen in silence and connect the heart with the mind. This is much more penetrating than just listening with the brain.

- Thoughts alone don't penetrate the soul.

- If we believe, that's the beginning of love, is it not? Faith is always love, always.

LESSON ELEVEN

Live to give: Giving and receiving are the same.

Fear-based thinking sees everything in terms of opposites. This part of your mind will try to convince you that giving and receiving have little connection. Today, you will see no such illusion. Instead, you will discover that there is no difference between giving and receiving and that whatever is truly worth having increases when given away.

Most everyone has had the experience of giving—perhaps going out of your way for your children or spouse, lending a hand to a neighbor, or donating to a cause you believe in—and the feeling of fullness and peace it brings. These seemingly small gestures whisper a truth to you: Giving and receiving are the same.

Giving and receiving are facets of the same thought and action. They occur together. It is with this thought that you will stop "giving" in order to "get," stop performing to receive approval, stop working toward a reward.

Today, regardless of the mood that you find yourself in, attempt to offer something to everyone—try compassion, or forgiveness—even to those with whom you may be upset. See how quickly peace enters into your mind. A new way of seeing yourself and the world will emerge as you focus your attention on giving—and receiving—compassion and forgiveness.

Begin your practice period today with the following prayer:

Dear God,

Today **show me** that **giving** and **receiving**
are the same. **Guide me** to give what **You** would have
me receive. **Demonstrate** to me that I will receive
whatever I **give now.**

∼ *Amen*

For the next five minutes, with your eyes closed, think about what you would offer to others that you would also like to have for yourself. For example:

- ✤ To all beings I offer quietness.

- ✤ To all beings I offer compassion.

- ✤ To all beings I offer understanding.

- ✤ To all beings I offer gentleness.

Repeat each gift slowly to yourself and then pause for a few moments. Expect to receive the gift that you just offered. You will receive what you give, be sure of this. If you prefer, you may focus your attention on one individual as the recipient of your gifts. However, be sure not to intentionally withhold your gifts from any individual or group, for you surely do not want to withhold them from yourself. Today's lesson can be applied to any situation at any time. If you are experiencing an upset, stop and repeat:

Dear God,

In this moment may I **offer the gifts** You would
have me experience, rather than the upset
that I have made.

∼ Amen

As you practice today's lesson you will see and experience direct results. Your progress can only be impeded by reverting to the old habit of fear-based thinking that results in scarcity-based generosity rather than abundance-based generosity. Say to yourself often: Giving and receiving are the same.

LESSON TWELVE

I create wealth by being generous with others.

Generosity will bring you all you want in life. Today, you will make the important decision to create wealth of all kinds by practicing abundance-based generosity. I define wealth as an experience, not a number on my bank statement. Wealth is an experience of happiness through receiving God's gifts in the present moment. This abundance is far from limited to the material possessions that we commonly use to define wealth. According to this definition of wealth, you could have a lot of stuff and a lot of money, and still not be wealthy. Or you could have a great deal and still believe in scarcity. Scarcity is the experience that results from the belief that there is not enough to go around. Whatever "it" is, you don't have enough of it.

Wealth that's measured by these criteria can never be satisfied. Begin by reminding yourself:

SCARCITY-BASED GENEROSITY IS FAULTY THINKING THAT EXISTS ONLY AS LONG AS IT GOES UNCHALLENGED AND UNRECOGNIZED FOR WHAT IT REALLY IS.

Today, you will banish scarcity-based generosity by, first, seeing it for what it is, and secondly, by practicing abundance-based giving. The powerful experience of giving the gifts that God would have you give replaces all old habits and ideas based on scarcity. Where there is an experience of the abundance of God through the act of generosity, there can not be a simultaneous experience of not having enough.

One obstacle you will face directly today is that the ego will say you are in need of defense, that nobody can be trusted, and that generosity is a luxury of the "wealthy," not a practice for those who are not. Many of us forget ever having an experience other than this. Perhaps you cannot remember a time when you were aware of God's love and abundance. Today, choose to create this experience by reversing the ego's way of thinking. Today, maximize your awareness of God and reduce the belief that you are separate from Him.

I ATTRACT WHAT I WANT IN LIFE BY BEING GENEROUS WITH OTHERS BECAUSE LIKE ATTRACTS LIKE. WHEN I ADOPT THE ATTITUDE OF GENEROSITY I OPEN THE DOORS TO ABUNDANCE IN ALL AREAS OF MY LIFE.

Imagine what a state of mind without separation, fear, greed, neediness, envy, and worry would be like. How would it feel? How would you see yourself and others? With your eyes closed during your practice periods, try to recall a time, even if it is the faintest memory, when there were no negative thoughts to interrupt your peace of mind. Maybe it was only for a minute, a very long time ago. It was a time when you knew you were loved and were safe in the moment. If no memory comes to mind, then make one up in your imagination by asking the above questions. Next, imagine that moment continuing until tomorrow, then the next day, and the next, expanding all the way to the end of time. Allow this peace to expand and multiply with each second that passes. Lastly, imagine how lovely it would be for every being on the planet to be able to remember the truth about who they are, and the powerful force this peace creates.

With each person you think about or meet today, remind yourself that you can either contribute to their memory of the peace of God, or you can choose to reinforce their belief in being separate from God. Remember: You are making this decision with every person that you meet, and your decision will reinforce what you believe about yourself.

I CREATE WEALTH BY BEING GENEROUS.

The experience of peace that results from today's lesson shows just a glimmer of the wealth, of all kinds, that is available to us. With generosity there can be no fear, no doubt, no defense, and no attack. With abundance-based generosity all pain of loss ends because we realize we can always choose to give and receive in each moment. Truth is like light. Once it comes into our mind it expands everywhere. All dark thoughts about not having enough vanish when we focus on the light of generosity and unity with God. The stock market can crash, but this does not separate us from God. Our jobs or homes can be lost, but these events do not separate us from God. Terrorists can attack, but they do not separate us from God. Anything can happen, but nothing can separate us from God.

WEALTH IS DETERRED WHEN I AM AFRAID OF THE PAST, OBSESSIVELY WORRY ABOUT THE FUTURE, AND WITHHOLD FROM OTHERS NOW.

Fear-based thinking assumes that "success" and "wealth" come and go. The ego believes that wealth and success can never be counted on. I have worked with many wealthy people who were afraid they would lose what they had and were obsessed with making more. In contrast, the abundance-based generosity of God-centered thinking does not disappear or suddenly change into something else. This kind of generosity creates success and wealth that do not wane with the ups and downs of the world. Why? Again, because the present moment is where the doorway to wealth exists, and giving God's gifts in this moment guarantees we will receive what we offer, and more.

I am not talking about what, when, or how much you give as much as I am talking about developing the *attitude* of generosity. I am not advising you to run to your bank and empty your account into someone else's. But it would be an obstacle to your wealth to withhold compassion from someone today because you were preoccupied with your past or future. Remember, *attitude* creates true wealth. Today, you are developing the attitude that will open the door to the abundance of God. Today, you will focus on creating wealth in all aspects of your life by having the attitude of generosity.

You may believe that the experience of wealth continues to escape your grasp. When you ask for wealth you are not asking for something that you do not already have; you are merely asking to recognize what is already there. Wealth *wants* to flow in your direction. Today, know that you are generous.

PRAYER FOR TRUE WEALTH

Dear God,

Today **lead me** to recognize that I already have
so much wealth to give right now—compassion,
understanding, kindness, prayer. When I **believe** I lack
anything to be happy, **help me** to turn to the attitude
of generosity. I welcome this attitude to enter
into every minute of the day.

∼ Amen

For as long as you hold a false view of generosity you will never experience true wealth. Remind yourself:

Error: I am separate from God. I need to constantly defend and hold on to what I have acquired. Because there is only a limited amount of what is valuable, I should be more concerned with getting then giving.

Truth: I am deeply connected with God and all that is, and all that ever will be. The gifts of God, such as love, compassion, kindness, and forgiveness, are always available to me to give, and this is what opens the door to the flow of wealth.

Today, focus on the truth. As you repeat the Prayer for True Wealth fear and scarcity will crumble and fall to dust and be blown away by the gentle breeze of generosity. Know that to be generous means to not purposely exclude anyone from the gifts you give. All the wealth that you want to create is contained within your attitude and is manifested through your acts of generosity. Your generous thoughts and actions today are the key to unlocking a present and future that is abundant. Love, compassion, kindness, and forgiveness are always available to you to give away, and each act of giving holds open the door to the flow of wealth from God.

∽ PATIENCE ∽

THOSE WHO ARE CERTAIN OF THE OUTCOME CAN AFFORD TO
WAIT, AND WAIT WITHOUT ANXIETY...THE TIME WILL BE AS
RIGHT AS IS THE ANSWER. AND THIS IS TRUE FOR EVERY-
THING THAT HAPPENS NOW OR IN THE FUTURE.

—*A Course in Miracles*

**PATIENCE MEANS THAT YOU HAVE CONFIDENCE IN THE
UNFOLDING OF YOUR LIFE.**

Patience is the attitude you assume when you trust God. You
trust that everything happens at the right moment, and that
you can learn from all situations. True patience comes from
knowing that right now is the only time there is, and each
instant is for giving love.

Many of us adhere to weekly, daily, even hourly schedules
and timetables, but do not recognize the irrationality of this.

Even when we do see the craziness of our lives, keep on doing the same things. We may find ourselves running from task to task, person to person, place to place, as quickly as possible, always thinking about what is next rather than what is *now*. We believe controlling our environment, other people, and social situations will bring peace of mind. We tend to become upset when things do not go according to plan.

Wouldn't it more rational to have an overall picture of our whole life but also live moment to moment, doing one thing at a time? Doesn't it make more sense to live lightly on the planet and not consume more than we have? Wouldn't it be more peaceful to accept than to control, to assist rather than dominate, to understand and embrace with patience rather than judge and condemn with force? When we see that every occurrence in our lives has the capability to teach us more deeply about love and trust in God, we can afford to be free of anxiety, frustration, and impatience. To be truly patient can be very difficult if your goal is always to control and never to accept what is.

EMBRACE THE PARADOX OF PATIENCE AND TIME BY HARNESSING THE POWER OF THE NOW.

I have over the years come up with some questions I routinely ask myself:

- Did you ever really wonder why you become impatient?

- Is it possibly because you are afraid and/or non-accepting of what is?

- If so, what is it that you might be afraid of?

- Why do you not want to be in the moment with what is?

- Is it because you fear the future will not be as you think it should be?

- Or are you afraid the past will repeat itself?

My answers to these questions have led me to see that fear and impatience are connected. Similarly, trust in God and patience are conjoined.

When we live according to the rigid reality of linear time—the false reality of past and future—we are bound to be fearful. This is because guilt about the past and worry about the future make sense to the fearful mind. But I have also found that:

WHEN I AM FEARFUL, GUILTY, AND WORRIED I AM VERY IMPATIENT.

Fear and guilt perpetuate the past and future. Together they create a place where patience is next to impossible. The ego uses anxiety to convince us that we cannot escape from time, and our best bet for happiness and safety is to try and control everything that happens. I know this from my own life.

God-centered thinking, prayer, and contemplation offer us the peace of the eternal moment in exchange for the guilty past and worrisome future we have created. Such an exchange shifts our focus away from the past and the future, and toward the present moment. This is the key to becoming a patient person. The following prayer puts this into action.

Dear God,

I gladly exchange what I have made
for what **You** created.

∽ *Amen*

I've battled with time for much of my life: endless deadlines, a long list of expectations, some self-imposed, others not. In the past, almost anything that delayed me from what I thought I was supposed to be doing was a source of great impatience. For example, if I found myself sitting in traffic that I had not anticipated, peace of mind was quickly exchanged for a tightening of my stomach and a clenching of my fists. I would curse who was in front of me if they were not driving exactly how I thought they should be. In recent years we all have become familiar with the term "road rage" in which impatience is taken to an extreme. Drivers shooting other drivers epitomize the irrationality of impatience, the seeds of which many of us have in our own minds.

Until about fifteen years ago my fight with time emerged in full force whenever I found myself waiting for people who were late. While growing up, I saw this same issue as a source of conflict for my parents. Departing on a vacation, for instance, was always an eventful experience, especially if there was an airplane departure involved. My father, always ready at least an hour before we needed to leave, usually began pacing and wringing his hands while my mother, usually running late, took her time. This combination did not make for a relaxed scenario. Rushing, despite having plenty of time, is as dysfunctional as always being late and unconcerned with the feelings of others. As an adult I tended to my father's form of irrationality over my mother's. Today, I feel that being on time is a good quality. But when I stop being aware and appreciative of the present moment, and lose the peace of mind that comes with it, I do not benefit. Although I was often on time, I used to be stressed, ornery, and miserable when I got there. Where is the value in that?

Now when I am running behind I am still tempted to get upset. However, more often than not I am able to look at what is right in front of me. It is easier to stop obsessing when I know I'm not going to make it to wherever it is I think I am supposed to be, so I show up where I am instead. This is a key factor of patience. Ask yourself:

- Do I want to be focused on—and anxious about—where I think I am supposed to be, or peacefully focused on where I am now?

- Do I want to be focused on what is happening right now, so I can react effectively and appropriately, or do I want to be obsessed with what I think should be happening right now and isn't?

Of all the prayers I know and practice, there is one from *A Course in Miracles* that has helped me to develop a patient presence in any situation life brings me:

I am here only to be truly helpful.

I am here to represent Him Who sent me.

I do not have to worry about what to say or what to do, because He Who sent me will direct me.

I am content to be wherever He wishes, knowing He goes there with me.

I will be healed as I let Him teach me to heal.

Not everyone is on the fast track that so many Americans are on. Living in a very small town in rural Mexico taught me a lot about the purpose of time. Over and over again I found things didn't happen at the speed I thought they were supposed to. From the outset, I was frustrated and impatient with many of the inconveniences. Something simple like making a phone call or acquiring money from a bank sometimes took an entire day.

Ironically, I went to Mexico to slow down and discover more peace of mind. But as you can imagine, by becoming anxious when things did not happen in a timely fashion was anything other than peaceful. Until about twenty years ago, my narcissism and grandiosity would have prompted me to react in one of these ways: I would have tried to get preferential treatment, convincing myself that I should not have to wait like everyone else; I would have lied, perhaps making up some sort of crisis; I would convince someone that I immediately had to have what I wanted; I would become manipulative and dishonest; I would have left, deeming the indigenous way incompetent and wrong; I would feel superior, and adopt an attitude that demanded attention.

All of the above had one thing in common: I thought I knew what I wanted and I believed the end justified the means. Decide right now that you will not continue to make the same mistakes I did. There is another way, and it is:

THE MEANS ENGENDER THE END.

I first heard the author Marianne Williamson say this, and I later realized that she was really talking about patience. When your approach to life is patient because you are God-centered, you create a life that is happy. Because like attracts like. If you are uptight and impatient, believing that the end justifies the means, don't expect any consistent happiness, even when you achieve the goal or get "the end" you thought you wanted. In contrast, when you believe that the means engender the end, and you adopt patience, your life will be change completely.

I went to Mexico intent on changing. While living there I began to realize there had to be another way to approach life's frustrations. I began to relax more and see that each situation had something to offer me. Trying to manipulate the outcome had made me blind to these gifts. Slowly, I learned to be with myself, to be with other people, rather than trying to control time. I came to know that the means engender the end. One particular experience stands out.

During my time in Mexico, I drove a beat-up 1971 Volkswagen camper that cost me five hundred dollars. I had a suntan from the knees down because I spent so much time under that van trying to fix it. After one particularly unsuccessful repair, I left the camper at a shop in a very small village to be worked on. The shop consisted of a palm-leaf lean-to and a couple of rusty chairs. I got frustrated when I realized nobody seemed to know much more than I did about the motor, and that wasn't much. Three men working on the vehicle were merely doing the same things I had already tried.

I made a real effort to put a hold on my escalating exasperation. Instead, I changed my mind—literally. I consciously decided that I was there for a purpose other than just to get my car repaired. I decided not to try to speed things up, or think of how much more fun I would be having if I were on the beach with my girlfriend. In the end the "small repair" took most of two days. Instead of faceless service workers, the men working on the car became my friends.

Although there is no grand conclusion to the story, it was a profound experience for me. My purpose was to surrender to the joy of being—really being—with whomever I was with, instead of thinking I should be someplace else doing something different with other people. The means (patience) engendered the end (peace and friendship).

This brings me to a phenomenon I like to call the paradox of patience. In fear-based thinking if you are too patient you will miss something vital that is someplace where you are not. Something important will happen when you are not present. The philosophy of "if I hurry up to get there, I will arrive that much sooner" sticks in the fear-based mind. But the problem is that even when you hurry to get there, you never seem to arrive. You rush to a series of appointments, rarely really being present with where you are. But something quite remarkable and paradoxical occurs when you develop patience: Patience produces immediate effects. The attitude of patience results in the experience of God's peace. *A Course in Miracles* illustrates this point:

> Now you must learn that only infinite patience produces immediate effects. This is the way in which time is exchanged for eternity. Infinite patience calls upon infinite love, and by producing results now it renders time unnecessary.

THERE IS CONTENTMENT TO BE FOUND IN A BUSY AND CRAZY WORLD.

For much of my life, prior to following a serious spiritual path, my personal motto could have been, "Happiness is knowing what is going to happen next." I felt most comfortable when I was in control of situations. I feared any situation that might not have a controllable outcome that I could manipulate.

Many of my control issues began when I was very young growing up in an alcoholic home. Arguments between my parents terrified me and often, I felt the situation could have easily escalated into physical violence or uncontrollable verbal attacks. I felt unsafe and unable to leave or control my world.

As a child, and later in adolescence, I tried to control these family conflicts and my personal relationships by adopting various physical problems. Irrationally and unconsciously, I believed if I were physically ill, the focus of attention would be on me rather than any other conflict between my parents. I would thus be able to control potential conflicts. Whether feigned or organically based, my ailments and injuries emerged from fear of conflict *and* intimacy, and a desire for more control.

In my life, fear and control have been the most damaging of my ego's cycles. Fear often has become manifest in my body, resulting in many serious health conditions. My own life experience, and many of my clients confirm this, has brought me to believe that many physical problems may actually have their origins in control issues.

For every one of the ego's damaging cycles, there is a God-centered alternative. By turning my life in the direction of God I have discovered health and healing. I define health as a state

of experiencing trust in God, and healing as an act of letting go
of fear.

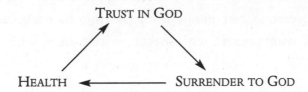

Notice that in the fear-based cycle of Fear-Control-Illness
there is little room or desire for patience. To the contrary, with
such a state of mind there is a constant struggle to control
events and outcomes. In the God-based cycle of trust in God-
Surrender to God-Health there is an immediate feeling of
peace. There is no fight with time, and no struggle with control. All is focused on the now. Patience just happens.

As a young adult I was uncomfortable with spontaneity. I
did not trust the unfolding of events in my life. I felt that knowing what was next, especially in terms of relationships, was of
the utmost importance. I did walk through life and take joy in
the spontaneous and creative aspects of existence. It was as
though I were attending a play as a member of the audience,
yet I would repeatedly get up and try to direct the production.
I was never fully satisfied with anything, not even with high
achievements. I thought if I could make every situation to my
liking I would have happiness.

I found, however, that I was not happy. Eventually, I came to
understand I needed to approach life differently. As a student of

many spiritual disciplines, I began to see that adopting an attitude of patience, based on trust in God, yields the release for the need to control. It is an ongoing process for me, but I have discovered that in relinquishing control I have a greater ability to be truly present with myself, with others, with God, and with life.

FIVE PRINCIPLES OF PATIENCE

- Know that within every life situation, including the most challenging, there is a valuable spiritual lesson to be learned. God brings us no useless occurrences or worthless interactions.

- Know that it is your beliefs about the purpose of a situation, not the "facts" about a particular situation, that determine your experience. If you believe the purpose is to make happen what you think you want, according to your time frame, you will not be patient or happy—regardless of the outcome. If you believe the purpose is to learn the lesson God wants you to learn, you will be patient and much, much happier—regardless of the outcome.

- Know that peace of mind comes from an awareness of Spirit in the moment. You cannot gain this awareness by being impatient with any aspect of yourself, other people, or the unfolding of your life.

❧ Know that to experience the most profound fragrance you would never rush a rose to bloom. Instead you would add nutrients to the soil, prune dead blossoms, and supply enough water. Treat yourself in the same manner: Make sure you deal honestly with yourself and others, let go of the past, and be patient and loving toward yourself and others.

❧ Know impatience brings conflict. When you need direction, your Higher Power, not the shrill voice of impatience, will lead you to success and peace.

MAKE EVERYONE YOUR SPIRITUAL TEACHER.

It never ceases to amaze me how fear-based thinking can work its way into our consciousness without our even realizing it. I think I would notice if twenty or thirty uninvited guests showed up in my living room, but I don't always recognize fearful or impatient thoughts in my mind.

I have made progress in becoming more aware of my negative thoughts, and turning to God for help in releasing them, but I don't always catch the fear-based thoughts when they first present themselves. By the time I recognize them they are already making quite a mess of my mind. One sure sign an uninvited thought is present is when I become impatient with someone—myself included. It may be the grocery clerk who is not ringing up items fast enough. It may be my kids not getting ready for school quickly enough. It may be that I think that I am making too many mistakes or taking too long at some task.

IMPATIENCE IS A TAP ON THE SHOULDER THAT SOMETHING IS NOT RIGHT IN YOUR THINKING. WHEN YOU ARE GOD-CENTERED AND TRUSTING, YOU ARE NOT IMPATIENT.

Whenever you are impatient with another person you are turning your back on a teacher God has offered for the sole purpose of helping you. This does not mean that every teacher will act like a kind and compassionate guru. In fact, some will appear to be on a mission to make your existence miserable. Remember:

THERE IS NO SITUATION OR PERSON THAT SEPARATES YOU FROM THE LOVE OF GOD. IN FACT, THERE IS NO PERSON WHO DOES NOT OFFER YOU THE OPPORTUNITY TO FIND GOD'S LOVE THROUGH OFFERING IT.

Even those whom you find most unbearable have something to teach you. For example, perhaps the rude, unfriendly person is here to teach you about kindness. Obviously it is easy to be kind to someone who is courteous and warm, but it is not so easy to extend yourself in kindness to someone who is, say, yelling at you.

BE WILLING TO BE PATIENT IN ALL CIRCUMSTANCES AND WITH ALL PEOPLE.

This does not mean you should allow yourself to be mistreated or stay in dangerous situations. It does mean, however, that you see the value in having the intention to extend empathy and compassion, because if you can do this you will automatically be patient.

Finding empathy and compassion—and thus, patience—when things are far from how you would like them, or when you are being treated poorly, is not an easy task. In such circumstances, I try to remember to ask myself:

What suffering has this person endured to make him act in this way?

During my first month of my first internship in clinical psychology, I worked with a young man named Nathan who was fifteen years old and had suffered moderate organic damage to both hemispheres of his brain. Two years before, a truck had struck him while he was riding his bicycle. His attention span was minimal. He often would lapse into very loud bursts of laughter or screams, or would repeat one phrase over and over. The left side of Nathan's body was partially paralyzed which caused a noticeably slow stride. But despite all this, his personality could still be seen. Through the months, glimpses of the "whole Nathan" revealed themselves now and then.

To be honest, Nathan and I got off to a rather slow start. I was new to the job and not really sure what the heck I was supposed to do. I was very aware that Nathan's "progress" as well as my own would be monitored by a supervisor. Frankly, part of me wanted him to do well so I would "look good."

As time went on I was able to let go of what "I was supposed to do" and became a bit more present with Nathan. But everything he did took at least five times as long as it once would have. One of my tasks was to help him become as self-sufficient as possible, for example, being able to go to a store without becoming confused, anxious, and disoriented. It all took time, and my increasingly busy schedule made me feel resentful and angry that Nathan was not making more rapid progress. I was embarrassed when he screamed in public. He was not getting better on my timetable and it was difficult to be patient with him when I had so many other patients to see and so much paperwork to do. Needless to say, with this attitude neither of us ended up feeling very good.

By the time my year-long internship was complete Nathan had made little progress. I believed this was due to the severity of his condition, not my approach, and I did not think too much or too often about Nathan after that.

Many years later, at a restaurant, I saw Nathan and another person having lunch together. I did not recognize him at first because he was not displaying any of the behavior—the loud laughter or bouts of screaming—that had so bothered me before. Nathan had gone to a group home that had one very remarkable counselor, Lisa, who was lunching with him that day. She had spent a great deal of time with Nathan. Their relationship did not ride on any conditions or expectations of improvement. It was clearly based on empathy and compassion—and, therefore, patience.

While Nathan went to the restroom, I spoke with Lisa. It was clear she really loved Nathan and had chosen to identify with the little glimpses of the "whole Nathan" rather than trying to "fix" the "problem Nathan." I thought of the hundreds of hours that they must have spent together and thought how remarkable they were.

I told Lisa how impressed I was with her. She said whatever patience she had she owed to Nathan. Lisa insisted that she was not the "professor of patience," but rather it was Nathan. "Can you imagine one day waking up and only being half as smart as you are now, and not being able to even tie your own shoes? Nathan is *my* teacher. I consider it an honor to spend time with him."

Nathan and Lisa, and countless others as well, have been great examples and patient teachers for me. Watching them interact I could see the qualities of patience and trust that seemed boundless. When I remember the lessons they gave me, I am well served.

SIX LESSONS OF PATIENCE

- Empathy + Compassion = Patience

- Whomever is in front of you is your teacher. We are all teachers and students to one another.

- Each moment you spend with another person is a precious gift. When you are with one person, you should not be with someone else or someplace else.

- Look to the heart of a person rather than to their behavior. Heart-to-heart communication can transcend impatience.

- Be gentle with yourself and others and you will move much further and faster.

- Walk when you could run. Sit silently when you could stand and stew. Listen when you could speak. Heal when you could harm. In these things you will find God's blessings for yourself and others.

LESSON THIRTEEN
Focusing on the present yields patience.

One thing that I am quite sure of is that when I am in a rush, or impatient in any way, I am not on the path to God. I think the present is called the present because it is a gift, a "present" perfectly chosen and wrapped by God.

TO BE PATIENT IS TO SEE ALL THINGS THROUGH THE PERCEPTION THAT ABIDES IN THE PRESENT MOMENT.

To accurately perceive another person, and to know how to effectively respond, you must see them only as they are now. This is equally true when looking at yourself. When you become impatient, you are, in fact, viewing life through past experiences, or with worry and anticipation of future events. When you are impatient you have decided that the present moment should be different than it is rather than accepting it's unfolding. Today, begin by reminding yourself: "What is, is." This is not a statement of resignation, but rather a first step toward an effective response to any circumstance in a positive way.

The truth is that the past has no reality in the present. It is over. Gone. The future is not yet here. Yet most of us consider it natural to use the past, or future anxiety, as the reference point for viewing the present. You may have adopted the belief that it is "natural" to try to control the future, and/or prevent the past from reoccurring, in order to make your life safe. Yet this approach is not natural. It is delusional. To become fully present to all the opportunities of life you must look upon yourself and others with no leftover judgments from the past or excessive worry about the future. The only way I know how to achieve this is through prayer. Start today with:

PRAYER FOR PATIENCE

Dear God,

Guide me today to **true patience,** the peaceful place
beyond my judgments from the past and my worry
about the future.

⤳ Amen

Peace will be yours today as you focus on the present. Patience is the miracle that occurs when you stop seeing the past and future as your only reality, and turn to God. You only become fearful, impatient, and controlling when you anticipate the future on the sole basis of your past experience, and ignore the lessons and opportunities available to you right now. Think how patient you would be if you decided:

THERE IS NO MOMENT, EVER, THAT DOES NOT EITHER HOLD AN OPPORTUNITY OR A LESSON THAT GOD IS OFFERING.

Today, you will make a very important decision. You will decide if this statement is true or false. I call it the "Moment of Truth" because you are deciding what the truth is about every moment of your existence. I fully trust in your decision, and I know your choice will make a major difference in your life. It is your "moment of truth." When you allow it to be the basis for all your interactions you rise above the past and the future, and by so doing you give yourself and others freedom. This decision can sever the chains that hold you back to all that God offers and wants for you. Remind yourself of it often, again and again, until it becomes part of your thinking.

PATIENCE IS THE OPPOSITE OF WORRY. THEY CANNOT OCCUR AT THE SAME TIME.

Today, focus on the present moment using the Prayer for Patience and find that patience brings you peace of mind and ends anxiety. Should you be tempted to excessively worry about a situation, or judge another person or yourself, repeat the following:

TODAY, I WANT FREEDOM AND SUCCESS. I TURN IN

Today, you will focus on three things: the Prayer for Patience, the Moment of Truth, and the mission statement above. The combination of these three practices will remind you to be patient in every situation, under any circumstances.

LESSON FOURTEEN

To be patient is to heal and be healed.

Patience and healing are intimately connected. So are impatience and sickness. Patience brings healing to your mind, whereas impatience brings dis-ease at all levels: emotionally, physically, spiritually. At the root of patience is the knowledge that you are not separate from God and that He is with you always, in all ways. This is also at the root of healing. Therefore, to be patient is to heal and be healed. With patience you heal your mind from the belief that you are alone and isolated. It may be helpful to revisit the definition of health and healing:

HEALTH IS A STATE OF EXPERIENCING TRUST IN GOD. HEALING IS LETTING GO OF FEAR. FURTHER, HEALING IS THE DECISION TO BE ONE AGAIN WITH GOD AND TO ACCEPT YOURSELF AND OTHERS AS SPIRITUAL BEINGS.

Because we all share an underlying common spiritual bond we are not healed alone. This is why you cannot experience healing while believing that you are separate from God, separate from other beings, better than or less than anyone else.

Patience is the sacred act that allows healing to take place. It is the "holy land of the mind" that allows the truth about yourself, others, and God to emerge unmarred by the ego and the web of despair it weaves with fibers made from the past and the future. To be healed is to accept God in the moment and to accept the underlying unity that always has been, and always will be. Patience and healing don't occur alone; they happen simultaneously in the present moment. Healing, forgiveness, and patience are one; as are sickness, judgment, and fear. Reaffirm this today:

Prayer for Health and Healing

Dear God,

I come to **You** today for healing. The **present moment**
is the altar to which I come to You, **humbly asking**
You to **free me** from all impatience and worry
I have carried for so long.

Show me that patience is **Your** gentle path to healing,
that health is a state of **trusting You,** and that healing
is letting go of fear of the past and future.

∼ Amen

Write this down and pray often today. Say it slowly, and listen intently. Remember, each person who is in your life, or comes into your life, offers you the opportunity for practicing this prayer. Adopt the attitude of patience and you will see the lessons and opportunities that you once overlooked.

Know that you do not experience healing alone, and be thankful to every situation and to every person that enters your life today. Gratitude will further reinforce patience. Remember, worry and judgment will not. As each new hour approaches, say to yourself:

TO BE PATIENT IS TO HEAL AND BE HEALED. PATIENCE WITH MYSELF AND OTHERS WILL REVEAL AN OPPORTUNITY OR A LESSON THAT GOD BRINGS TO ME TODAY.

Today, you will focus on two important tasks. First, you will make the commitment to see the true nature of health and healing. Secondly, you will make the decision to heal your mind by recalling the Prayer for Health and Healing. Thirdly, you will remind yourself hourly of what patience will reveal.

One last tip for today: Focus for a few minutes on your breathing. When you are calm and patient your breath is naturally fluid and deep. In contrast, when you are impatient and anxious your breath is short and shallow. Begin your hourly practice by focusing on your breathing. Consciously deepen and slow each respiration. Should you find yourself "off track" during the day, before you even repeat the lesson to yourself or say the prayer, spend a few moments redirecting your breathing.

∼ OPEN-MINDEDNESS ∼

IF YOU HOLD FIRMLY TO SOME SET OF BELIEFS OR OTHER,
YOU LOOK AT EVERYTHING THROUGH THAT PARTICULAR PREJU-
DICE OR TRADITION; YOU DON'T HAVE ANY CONTACT WITH
REALITY... IF YOU HAVE NO PREJUDICE, NO BIAS, IF YOU ARE
OPEN, THEN EVERYTHING AROUND YOU BECOMES EXTRAORDI-
NARILY INTERESTING, TREMENDOUSLY ALIVE.

—J. Krishnamurti, *Think on These Things*

THE TIME HAS COME TO VALUE SPIRITUAL EXPERIENCE.
To many of us, being open-minded is vastly undervalued. Our
education system places primary emphasis on teaching children how to be critical, analytical, comparative, objective, logi-
cal, and categorical. What is missing is the development of
something that is a departure from many of these traits, and
this is open-mindedness.

Open-mindedness is not the same as objectivity, and the

word "objective" is one that stands out for me. Our culture has become reliant upon, if not addicted to, the idea that being objective is superior over the subjective spiritual experiences. How much money you have, for example, or what kind of career you pursue, is valued more than the depth of your inner experience of self and Spirit. If you make a decision and someone asks, "How did you decide that?" you may feel compelled to provide a chronology that documents your ability to think objectively. Those who make decisions by also including their intuition might be seen as intellectually weak or "out there." A manager who says, "I hired this person for the following five reasons," is seen as rational, reasonable, responsible—a practical decision-maker—versus someone who says, "I hired this person not only because of their qualifications, but also because I feel an intuitive trust in them."

One thing that I have become quite sure of is that in virtually every situation there is almost always more than meets the eye. There was a time in history when everyone believed the world was flat. Prior to the discovery of the New World, the insanity of someone setting a course for the edge of the Earth was laughable. I remember this when meeting people who do not value what I do and teach. I have set my mind on a course toward higher awareness and the peace of God: A New World that is God-centered rather than fear-based. To those who believe there is no such place it makes little sense. However, I still choose to set sail in this direction each and every moment of each and every day.

That which is objective is "real"—measurable, tangible, and observable. It is not necessarily bad information, just limited. The spiritual encompasses the intimate and internal experiences that defy conventional ideas about reality, measurement, and observation. Spiritually-based information is communicated to us when we are open-minded and receptive to more than the objective. It is communicated by, but is not limited to, our emotions, perceptions, thoughts, feelings, intuitions, inspiration, hunches, creativity, values, preferences, dreams, and all that makes each of us more than just flesh and bones.

Throughout history, the great spiritual teachers operated from something other than objective data. They were open to something much larger than their own minds, and this sensitivity and receptivity were at the source of their vocation. Each one of us can live in the same way. Try thinking about it like this:

OBJECTIVE INFORMATION ALONE CAN BUILD WALLS THAT BLOCK US FROM SEEING WHAT IS POSSIBLE AND WHAT THE TRUTH IS.

But:

OPEN-MINDEDNESS ALLOWS FOR A POWER GREATER THAN OURSELVES TO REACH US, INSPIRE US, GIVE US PURPOSE, AND SEE THAT NOTHING IS IMPOSSIBLE.

Open-mindedness is the invitation to your Higher Power to come into your mind. Conversely, when you only rely on objective information you are posting a "No Trespassing" sign, and this makes it very difficult for your Higher Power to reach you.

I believe that spiritual experiences are our source of "aliveness." The truth about who we are does not lie in objective information: It lies in our spiritual experiences, the ebb and flow of our inner sea—a sea that flows with the waters of Spirit and fills each person with wonder and mystery. When we rely on objective information and are closed to the spiritual, we deny our limitless relationship to God. You are standing on the beach with your back to the sea, saying it does not exist. Turn around.

PEOPLE WANT TO BE UNDERSTOOD, NOT ATTACKED.

When we are open-minded we believe there is more than one way to see a situation, more than one way to do things, more than one ideology, and so forth. Of course, this has value to all our relationships, in that we will seek to understand rather than criticize. It also creates a space for our Higher Power to enter our thinking. When we are closed-minded we become very attached to being right and then stop wanting to understand.

To be open-minded does not mean that you have to be in agreement. It means that you want to understand and respect varied points of view and opinions. Many people mistakenly believe that to say "I understand you" means the same as "I agree with you." Rather, being open-minded says: "I will do my best to listen, understand, and not attack."

The way your relationships manifest are like waves continually advancing and receding on the shore. Each wave is different than the last, but of the same waters. The shape of the shore is ever changing. Do you believe, after watching a succession of waves, that you understand the nature of *all* waves? Probably not. In the same way, each moment brings with it a new, wonderful, and unique experience.

Let me clarify further with a personal example: I believe that I know my daughters very well. When I think about it, I probably know thousands of details about them. Yet if I take this accumulated information and say to myself, "I now know my daughters completely and totally," I have made a grave mistake. As are each of you, my daughters are much more than an accumulation of information and experiences. In order to stay fresh and open-minded in my relationship with them, I try to always remember that I don't know the nature of the next wave no matter how long I sit on the beach and watch the surf.

Fear-based thinking uses memory, which is selective, to become closed-minded. It uses this closed and selective memory as a way of predicting the future and categorizing people and experiences. Within this closed mind we begin to develop categories of information, or schemas (a set of beliefs that we look through to determine how we see something). We then tend to want to fit new information into these schemas, rather than see things for how they are in the moment.

In Carmel, near where I live today, there used to live a man by the name of Max. When I was growing up I spent summers in Carmel, and even then Max was quite elderly. I was surprised when Max came to visit me at the hospital where I was on medical staff. He had heard I was back living in town and he wanted to visit me. I had not seen Max since I was about twelve. Amazingly, he looked exactly as he had more than twenty years earlier.

Max walked on Carmel beach every day for over five decades. Each day he tended to the shoreline as though it was his own back yard, lovingly picking up trash, smiling and speaking to anyone he met. Talking with Max at the hospital that day, I realized that his enthusiasm for life, as well as the beach, was remarkable—much like that of a child seeing the ocean for the first time. He had nothing but eager and open anticipation each time he went. I do not think Max ever saw the same shell, boulder, or tide pool in the same way twice.

From Max I learned about open-mindedness, and I learned about youth. He showed me that age has nothing to do with chronological time. Youth is the ability to walk through life with an open mind—with an eye for the miracles and beauty that are in front of us each day.

Disappointingly, many of us are not happy, even though we say we desperately want to be. I believe we are unhappy for the simple reason that we are unaware of the love in our hearts and minds put there by God. We are unaware because we are too busy maintaining the complicated process of keeping a closed mind. Believe me, being closed-minded takes a lot of energy! Open-mindedness, on the other hand, takes very little effort. In fact, it energizes instead of drains us. As Max walked his beloved beach and smiled at each person he met, he taught by example that love fills our hearts as soon as we remove the barriers between ourselves and other people, nature, and God.

WHEN WE CEASE TO BE CLOSED-MINDED, WE ARE FREE TO SIMPLY ENJOY THE BEAUTY OF SOMETHING OR SOMEONE WITHOUT CATEGORIZING, ATTACKING, ARGUING, OR DISTANCING. THIS REMOVES THE BAR-RIERS TO GOD.

Most of us, including myself, have a very difficult time with this. Being closed-minded is a habit that our minds have relied on for years, thinking it made the world safe. When we observe something, our mind seems to want to conclude: "This is similar to the other one I saw." "Experience tells me this is of no use." "I already know this is good, that is bad." When we open our minds we release them from prejudice. We allow what we see to describe itself to us, rather than letting our preconceived thoughts and past experiences define it. This is a profound difference. There is no more singularly powerful change in our thinking than wanting to be completely open-minded. The next time you are going to meet with someone, say the following prayer beforehand:

Dear God,

Help me to let go of all I think I know so that I can see what **You** would have me see.

∼ Amen

TO HAVE AN OPEN MIND, YOU MUST QUIET YOUR MIND.

For a while I was living in a house with a satellite dish for television reception, and at certain times the "news feed" (raw footage with no commentary by an anchorperson) would come over the air. I found that my mind was so used to being told what was going on and what to see, as in a regular news broadcast, that I became easily bored with the news feeds. My mind had become too lazy to observe and listen and interpret for itself in the moment.

Open-mindedness occurs when you turn down the volume of your thoughts and experience what you are seeing. You might consider trying to develop your skills in observation and listening without commentary. It can be quite a difficult task for the mind that has become accustomed to constant input, but it is a most worthwhile skill to have. Just observe, experience, and discover. Try a variation of the previous prayer, such as:

Dear God,

Help me to quiet my mind so that I can see what **You**
would have me see.

~ *Amen*

Then, simply observe the world around you: the trees, the
animals, people talking, laughing, crying. Something quite
remarkable will happen deep inside you. Your heart will
become activated. What you experience is interpreted by your
heart rather than from your always-busy intellect. When you
are open and observing the world God would have you see,
everything becomes miraculously interesting and amazingly
alive.

FOR AN OPEN MIND, LET GO OF YOUR ATTACHMENTS.

Have you ever looked openly and honestly at how attached
you have become to beliefs, to material things, and to outcomes in your life? It is difficult to do so because fear-based
thinking tells us we need each and every one of them in order
to be happy. And fear-based thinking fears and avoids any type
of loss.

To be open-minded we must free ourselves from the attachments of the ego and heal our fear of loss. Another variation of
the Prayer for Open-Mindedness is useful here:

Dear God,

Help me to release my attachments, and trust that **You** are with me **always,** even during loss, so I can see what **You** would have me see now.

⌒ *Amen*

Attachments keep you from God because you think there are certain criteria that *must* be met for you to be happy. Inordinate attachment happens when you believe a particular person, idea, ideology, or object will make you happy. When you are willing to turn your attachments over to your Higher Power, you recognize that attachment to a particular thing enslaves you to it. You fear its loss, and your options of spontaneity, guidance, and unencumbered choice diminish or even disappear.

The mind that fears loss does not want to be questioned about its attachments. When attached to a particular level of physical and/or emotional comfort, a certain belief, an established habit, or even to a specific geographical location, the mind becomes encased in defenses. Ultimately, it will do almost anything not to suffer loss. This thinking keeps you from what is important: Allowing your mind to be open and marvel at all creation. Attachments do not allow for this. With each attachment you move a little further away from the ability to experience inner simplicity.

Developing inner simplicity, which is the state of not having so many attachments, is like walking in a beautiful garden, not an elaborate or ornate garden, just a beautifully simple one: cleanly raked, the flowers in bloom, perhaps a wind chime in the distance. Inner simplicity rests in the mind not weighted down with the bitterness of past resentments, or clogged with endless fears about the future. Prayer and meditation offer a path toward such simplicity. The non-attached mind is available for genuine intellectual freedom because it is not full of preconceived and rigid ideas. Attachments make it difficult to discover and explore your self and your spiritual path. One thing I am reminded of almost daily is that it is hard to travel to the depths of my self, my relationships with other people, and God, when I cling to inflexible judgments or limiting beliefs. Without prayer and meditation this freedom would be impossible for me.

EVERY DAY, I WILL VOW TO OPEN MY MIND AND OPEN MY HEART.

After reading a number of self-help books, a friend asked me recently, "Does anybody ever tell us what letting go really is or how to do it?" There is nothing complicated about letting go. For example, if you grabbed the handle of a hot pan on the stove, I doubt very much if you'd think about how to let it go, you'd just do it. There is a pretty quick response between "hand burning real bad" and "let go." This response needs to be developed between the awareness of "thoughts injuring" and "let go." Letting go is simple once you fully recognize what is injuring you.

To get a better feel for what the experience of holding onto attachments vs. letting go brings you, try the following exercise: Make fists of your hands, closing them as tightly as possible. What do you feel as you look at them? Then relax your hands, making them as supple and open as possible. What do you feel? Can you feel the difference in these two postures, how they create two different experiences? It certainly takes more effort to keep your hand tightly closed in a fist than it does to relax it into an open palm. (Have you ever seen an image of Jesus or Buddha, or any other spiritual teacher, with clenched fists, tightly crossed arms, or furrowed brow? Probably not. They are usually portrayed with an open-handed, palm-up gesture.) What is true of your hands is true of your mind. Although many of us grew up being encouraged to keep a closed mind, we rarely question the energy that it takes to maintain it. Nothing depletes your energy more than being closed-minded and guarded and afraid.

It is important to recognize the connection between having a closed mind and having a closed heart. When you begin to open your mind, you make room for broader and different ideas and perceptions. This in turn allows your heart to open. Because closed-mindedness is caused by fear, it limits your loving heart. When ideas are free to come and go in an open mind, you are free to give and receive from your open heart.

I recently asked a friend what she was doing one day. She replied, "Not much, just walking around reminding myself I don't really know much so I can turn to God for answers."

I WILL HEAL OLD WOUNDS AND RELEARN TO OPEN MY HEART AND MIND TO SPIRIT.

I hope you encourage your children to explore and communicate with an open mind and open heart. Unfortunately, some parents douse the sparks of their child's spiritual connection to God with water from the well of fear. Their children hear, "Don't ever tell me I am wrong." "Do as I say, not as I do." "Shut up." "You don't know anything." "You're stupid." "Where do you get such dumb thoughts and ideas?" "Who do you think you are?" These statements teach children to close their minds and to become guarded and fearful, intolerant and defensive. The good news is that, as adults, we can unlearn old messages that caused us to close off and shut down. We can open ourselves to the world of endless diversity and love that lives within and around each of us. Let's talk about how.

When I was in practice as a psychologist I spent thousands of hours working with people who had grown up with varying degrees of verbal and physical abuse. I have come to believe that working through childhood issues—talking about them, crying about them, being angry about them, understanding them, and forgiving what happened—is extremely important. I have also discovered that it is insufficient. I believe that prayer must be included in any approach to heal childhood wounds, especially in cases of severe abuse.

This section cannot take the place of a psychotherapist, group counseling, a meditation retreat, a spiritual mentor, or a good friend. But it can offer you two things: First, a simple prayer that can greatly facilitate healing, and second, a series of questions designed to bring up ways you may have been shut down as a child that have resulted in being closed-minded and closed-hearted. The purpose of raising these issues is not to relive them but to heal from them through reflection and prayer.

Practice the following prayer consistently over a period of months to help you initiate healing. The questions that follow it will allow you to make sense of the wounds from your past.

PRAYER TO HEAR GOD TELL YOU WHO YOU ARE

Dear God,

I ask You to **lift the veil** of pain from my past
and **teach me** throughout the day who I am.
Give me Your words in place of those of others,
past and present, who would have me be less than I am.
It is only **Your** words I choose to hear.
It is with **Your** words I choose to define myself.

∼ Amen

Like so many things, I have come to see that an individual's level of open-mindedness is set very early in life. There are many things that lead us to being closed-minded, but most have to do with how our parents (or primary caregivers) raised us. For this reason, each of us would do well to explore our own personal history. It is important to know, however, that the purpose is not to blame our parents or other people. Our task is to observe the impact of the past on our level of open-mindedness *today* so that we may heal and define ourselves, and our purpose, through God. The path to being open-minded is not through blame.

Below is a list of some of the primary issues and obstacles phrased in the form of questions so they can be personalized for self-reflection. Note that certain categories overlap, and some questions could easily appear in more than one category. Take your time. No matter how many "yes" answers you give, remember that healing your heart and opening your mind is always possible through the Prayer to Hear God Tell You Who You Are.

Emotional Growth

1. Were your parents emotionally inconsistent?

2. Were your parents sporadic with support and discipline?

3. Were your parents non-supportive of your individuality and uniqueness?

4. Were either of your parents chemically dependent?

5. Did either of your parents physically strike you?

6. Was either parent overprotective, controlling, or emotionally manipulative?

7. Was workaholism present in your family?

8. Was one parent overly dominant?

9. Did you witness spousal abuse between your parents?

10. Were you told not to cry, or were certain emotions seen as a sign of weakness?

11. Did either parent tend to rage or blow up in anger?

12. Was physical affection generally withheld, or used in a manipulative or uncomfortable manner, in your family?

13. Did you feel that either parent was emotionally distant or unavailable most of the time?

14. Did you feel you had to gauge what you said according to your parents' moods?

Intellectual Growth

1. Were either of your parents rigid or prejudiced in their views of others?

2. Were either of your parents extremely opinionated, insinuating that other family members were stupid if they did not agree with him or her?

3. Did either parent put others down in order to feel superior?

4. Did your parents withhold encouragement and positive reinforcement when you expressed your opinions?

5. Did your parents disapprove when you expressed your own thoughts and ideas that differed from theirs?

6. Did your parents push you to an extreme to perform to certain high standards?

7. Were you ever called stupid or dumb?

8. Did the nonverbal messages in your family suggest that you were different and didn't belong?

9. Were you embarrassed in school to speak up in class? Did you fear having a wrong answer?

10. Did you tend to get in trouble if you challenged a parent or said "no" to a parental demand?

11. Were you afraid of one or both of your parents?

Social Interaction and the Development of Healthy Sexuality

1. Was either parent fearful of sexuality, either yours or theirs?

2. Did your parents have expectations on what "type" of friends and social life you should have?

3. Was either parent seductive towards you, either covertly or overtly?

4. Was either parent socially or monetarily competitive with others?

5. Was either parent racist or bigoted in any way?

6. Did your parents emphasize outer appearance more than inner feelings?

7. Was there a great deal of emphasis in your family on social status?

8. Were you ever shamed in public by either parent?

9. Was sex and sexuality ever discussed in your family? Were they talked about only in joking or degrading ways?

10. Did your parents look to you to bring social acceptance to the family?

11. Was your choice of friends criticized on a continual basis?

12. Did either parent ever socially embarrass you?

13. Were you made to be afraid of other people or new situations?

14. When you made a mistake, was it usually met with ridicule and/or punishment?

15. Was being alone difficult for you?

16. Was being with others difficult for you?

Spiritual Growth

1. In your family was one religion seen as superior to others?

2. Was God or spirituality denied in your family?

3. Was God used as a way to make you behave through fear of God?

4. Was the concept of sin used to induce guilt and control behavior?

5. Was morality used as a means to judge other people as being good or bad?

6. Were fear and intimidation used as forms of discipline?

7. Were you required to think and believe in a certain way about God and spirituality?

8. Were questions of a spiritual nature discouraged?

It is important to take some time on each of the "yes" answers. Write about them in a journal. Think about them. Feel them. Talk to friends. If you wish, seek professional help. Perhaps talk with your parents. Lesson Sixteen is an exercise specifically geared to work through whatever issues arise from the questions. But most importantly, practice the Prayer to Hear God Tell You Who You Are.

The point of this phase is to, a) bring the aspects that lead to a closing of your heart and mind into your conscious awareness, to b) turn to your Higher Power and ask them to be lifted, and to c) ask your Higher Power to offer you a spiritual awareness of yourself.

For many of us this will be neither an easy nor a brief

process. It takes faith that the journey towards openness is a worthwhile one.

I know that in my life the search for the aspects of my self that remain closed and afraid continues. Sometimes, when I least expect it, a memory or feeling will surface. This is another opportunity for me to turn to prayer to discover the truth about myself. It *always* leads me to more openness to God and clarity about my life. Always.

I sometimes liken my personal quest for open-mindedness to keeping my windows clean, something that needs to be done on a continual basis. My history has yielded a fair share of "yes" answers. After years of inner work and prayer, I am happy to say that I now feel my relationship with my parents is the best it has ever been. Most importantly, I realize that this peace of mind has *not* been a result of my parents "making amends" for their "wrongs." It is a result of identifying and working through and breaking down the walls to openness that are in my mind, and then turning to prayer to seek and receive a new God-centered perception of myself and others.

LESSON FIFTEEN

Let me see things as they really are.

When you look through a tinted lens, you see a tinted world. In this way, when you are looking through the lens of the past, you cannot see anything as it truly is *now* at this moment. This includes yourself, others, God, the entire world. Many of us have developed the habit of using our past experiences to determine the value of what is occurring in the present. In doing so we miss the essence of what we are actually experiencing.

Today, you will begin to develop the skill of being open to the true nature of who or what is in front of you. At first, the idea that what you see might not be there may sound like gibberish. The lesson of "let me see things as they really are," implies that you do not see things as they are and have made them into something they are not. To the closed mind, this concept can produce uncomfortable feelings. Indeed, you may find yourself resistant to even entertaining such an idea because you have become so attached to seeing the world as you do. Fortunately, you do not have to worry about being resistant, or not understanding. The smallest effort today will allow God to enter your mind and show you something other than the world you have made and call "real." The goal of each lesson is to practice applying the idea and to then experience the effects. It is not necessary even to fully understand the idea behind each lesson or to be perfect in its application. Each minute that you practice today's lesson will open your mind a little more to what is and always will be: God's love in the eternal moment. Begin with the following prayer:

PRAYER TO SEE THINGS AS THEY ARE

Dear God,

If I am upset in any way and am not experiencing
Your peace and compassion, it is because
I am seeing something that is not there
in place of what **You** would have me see.
I **humbly ask** You to let me see things as they really are.

⤳ Amen

With your eyes still closed, admit that you don't see things as they really are. Express your wish to turn to God. Then, open your eyes and look around you. Apply the idea of "I don't see anything as it is now" to whatever your eyes land on. You needn't include everything, yet you must not consciously or deliberately exclude anything or anyone. For example, you might look around and say:

"I do not see this computer as it is now."

"I do not see this telephone as it is now."

"I do not see this arm as it is now."

Begin with things that are near to you and then gradually extend your visual range outward. If you wish, you may close your eyes and apply the lesson to whoever comes to mind.

"I do not see my mother as she is now."

"I do not see myself as I am now."

"I do not see my daughter as she is now."

End your practice session by looking at the objects, or thinking about the people, while repeating a shorter version of the Prayer to See Things as They Are. Go slowly. Allow plenty of time to listen to God before you continue.

Dear God,

In place of what I think I know, I **humbly ask** You to let
me see things as they really are.

~ *Amen*

In addition to your usual practice, four fifteen-minute practice periods are recommended today. Should you encounter any challenges during the day, quickly turn to God and say:

Dear God,

I want to see this person only as they are now, with my
thoughts unencumbered by the past and unafraid of the
future. Please **show me** what **You** would have me see.

~ *Amen*

Similarly, if you encounter a situation you are less than peaceful about, remember to turn to God and say:

Dear God,

I want to see this situation with the purpose **You**
would have me see, unencumbered by the past,

and unafraid of the future. Please **show me**
what purpose **You** would have me see.

～ *Amen*

LESSON SIXTEEN

**I am determined to see things as God
would have me see them.**

Today's lesson is a continuation and expansion of the
last one. Today, you will further your commitment to open-
mindedness with determination. To be determined is to set
your mind steadfastly in a direction. True determination is an
extremely powerful tool that you have at your disposal. Today,
you will set your mind steadfastly towards God by exercising
your determination. In addition to your usual practice, five
practice periods of five minutes each would be ideal.

The goal today is a two-step process of "bringing up" and
"letting go." You will consciously bring up the obstacles to
open-mindedness in order to then release them to your Higher
Power for healing. In each of the practice periods you may
begin by repeating the lesson to yourself:

I AM DETERMINED TO SEE THINGS AS GOD WOULD HAVE
ME SEE THEM.

Then close your eyes and ask the question: "What memories or situations from the past or the present, or anticipated

events in the future, bring up uncomfortable feelings for me that get in the way of my peace of mind?"

Try not to exclude anything that comes to mind, even if you feel it is only a mild annoyance. Also, even if you want to, for the purpose of this lesson don't allow your mind to dwell on certain memories, current situations, or people that seem to be disturbing you. Remember that whatever comes to mind is the subject of today's lesson. Don't worry if this seems insignificant at first, or if it seems overwhelming. Also, you may come across angry and attacking thoughts. Remind yourself that you can let these thoughts in, *without acting on them,* and then practice the rest of the lesson. Today, you will have the opportunity for transformation.

As you search your mind for obstacles to openness, hold each one in your mind as you say to yourself:

"I am determined to see _____ (name of person) as God would have me see them."

"I am determined to see _____ (specify the situation) as God would have me see it."

In this lesson, it is helpful to utilize your breath. On the inhale, as you think about a person or situation, say one of the above phrases. On the exhale, let go of whatever your upset or concern is. Feel yourself relax as you do. Do this for several minutes. Then spend some time listening to how it is God would have you see the person or situation. Initiate this phase with the prayer:

PRAYER OF DETERMINATION AND RECEPTIVITY

Dear God,

My determination has opened the door for
You to enter my mind.

I am now ready to hear **Your** wisdom and guidance.

~ *Amen*

If your mind stubbornly returns to the negative, reinitiate the breathing exercise for a few breaths, and then repeat the prayer.

Feel free to expand on the lesson as you see fit, especially to create a positive alternative to painful experiences in your past. For example, after applying the above practice to the question: "Were your parents non-supportive of your individuality and uniqueness?" you might add a positive statement of affirmation you receive from your Higher Power, such as: "My uniqueness is important and deserves to be supported."

It takes determination and practice and patience to reverse the old ways of seeing and perceiving. Today, you will cease to carry the dead weight of the past—guilt, resentments, anger, and other unforgiving thoughts. Today, you will to turn to God to begin to loosen all that holds you back from being fully alive and realizing your full potential. Remind yourself often:

ANY THOUGHTS OTHER THAN THE THOUGHTS GOD
GIVES ME ARE FALSE. LET ME SEE THINGS AS GOD
WOULD HAVE ME SEE THEM TODAY, AND DO MY BEST TO
LIGHT THIS VISION IN ALL WHOM I MEET.

AFTERWORD

~

I thought a good deal about how to end this book. I began to write what I wanted to say. I wrote at some length, somehow losing the simplicity of what I wanted to say in far too many words. I threw away what I had written and went for a walk. With each step I prayed to be given the words when I next sat down to write. On my way back, walking by the river near my home, I knew I would be given what I asked for.

Sitting down at my computer, the words of Joseph Campbell came to me the moment I began to type. He says all I wish to leave you with in ten words or less.

THE PRIVILEGE OF A LIFETIME IS BEING WHO YOU ARE.

— Joseph Campbell

Index

~

A

Abundance, 87
  generosity based on, 94, 95–96,
    106–107
Acceptance
  of guilt, 55–56
  of joy, 46
  of shame, 55–56
  tolerance and, 23–24
Agreement, 138
Aliveness, 138
Anger
  at childhood issues, 147
  family counseling and, 80
  forgiveness and, 9
  teenagers and, 78
Arrogance, intolerance and, 18
The Art of Loving (Fromm), 93
Assertiveness, gentleness and, 34
Attachments, 66–70
  letting go of, 145–146
  open-mindedness and, 143–144
  prayer for release of, 70, 144
Attacking, open-mindedness and,
    138–141

Attitude
  of generosity, 107–108
  of patience, 111
Avoidance, 78

B

Beauty, joy and, 52–53
Behavior, thought and, 71
Blame
  family counseling and, 80
  self-esteem and, 77
Breathing, patience and, 133
Bringing up the past, 158–159
Buddha, 48, 49, 146

C

Calls for love, 75–76
Campbell, Joseph, 163
Changing your mind, 71–72
Child abuse, 147
Childhood issues, healing of,
    147–153
Children
  closed-mindedness, teaching, 147
  prayer for healing issues of, 148

H

Hafiz of Shiraz, 15
Hands, openness of, 146
Harmful behavior, 35
Healing
    childhood issues, 147–153, 148
    with gentleness, 39–42
    gentleness and, 42
    open-mindedness and, 147–148
    patience and, 131–133
    prayer for, 132
Healing the Addictive Mind, 27
Health, 120–121
Henka, 34–35
Higher Power. *See* God
High productivity, 39
Holidays, 83–84
    defensiveness, reducing, 84–86
Honesty, 1–14
    forgiveness and, 5–9
    grievances and, 10–14
    tolerance and, 17

I

Impatience, 20, 23
    conflict and, 123
    dis-ease and, 131
    road rage, 114
    sources of, 112–114
    uninvited thought and, 123–124
Inner beauty, 53
Inner simplicity, 144–145
Intellectual growth issues, 150–151
Intention of generosity, 98
Intolerance, 18–19
    degree of, 20
Intuition, 34–35

J

Jesus, 48, 146
Joy, 43–63
    acceptance of, 46
    beauty and, 52–53
    forgiveness and, 61–62
    gentleness and, 43–44
    inherent internal joy, 45
    limiting visions of, 60–61
    Mother Teresa on, 99–101
    prayers for, 46, 62
    and present moment, 44
    service and, 52
    vision, joy-inspired, 59–62
    walking meditation for, 48–49
Judgment, 16. *See also* Tolerance
    gentleness and, 30, 36

K

Kindness, 87
    appreciation for, 91
    prayer for, 91–92
Krishnamurti, J., 135

L

Letting go, 145–146
    determination and, 158
Listening for gentleness, 36–39
Loneliness, holidays and, 83–84
Love, 54–55
    appreciation for, 91
    communication and, 75–76
    comparisons and, 88
    defensive behavior and, 75, 76
    of God, 58
    gratitude and, 88–89
    Mother Teresa on, 99–101

Suffering
   generosity and, 97
   over-identification with, 51
Suicide, teenage, 76
Sunday Lesson, xvi, xvii
   role of, xx
Survival tools, gentleness and, 32

T
Tardiness, conflict and, 114–115
Teachers, people as, 124
Teenagers
   emotional distance and, 77–80
   suicide/pregnancy, 76
Think on These Things
      (Krishnamurti), 135
Thought. *See also* Negative thoughts
   responsibility for, 71–72
   uninvited thought, 123–124
Thrill-seeking behavior, 44–45
Time and patience, 115–116
Trungpa, Chögyam, 29
Tolerance, 15–27
   acceptance and, 23–24
   desire for, 19–20
   fault-finding, effect of, 24–27
   honesty and, 17
   practicing, 21–23
   prayer for, 21

Trust
   in God, xii–xiii
   harmful behavior and, 35
Truth, generosity and, 107, 109
Tulka, Tarthang, 1
Tutu, Archbishop Desmond,
   48

U
Understanding, 138–141
Unhappiness, xii, 140–141
   grievances and, 11
Unifying goals, 73–74
Uninvited thought, 123–124

V
Vision, joy-inspired, 59–62

W
Walking meditation, 48–49
Wealth
   from generosity, 104–109
   prayer for true wealth, 108
Williamson, Marianne, 117
Work, joy and, 45–46
Worry, patience and, 130

Y
Youth, 140

As a recognized leader in psychology and human potential, Dr. Jampolsky has served on the medical staffs and faculties of respected hospitals and graduate schools. He has consulted with management and CEOs of businesses of all sizes, and has contributed to the spiritual growth of countless individuals, groups, and organizations around the globe.

❧ **Dr. Lee Jampolsky welcomes your interest in his work. For his free daily words of wisdom online and ways you can interact directly with Lee, please visit his website at www.DrLeeJampolsky.com.**